INTENTIONAL
CONVERSATIONS

Published by Familius LLC, www.familius.com

Familius books are available at special discounts for bulk purchases for sales
promotions or for family or corporate use. Special editions, including personalized
covers, excerpts of existing books, or books with corporate logos, can be created in
large quantities for special needs. For more information, contact Premium Sales at
559-876-2170 or email specialmarkets@familius.com.

Library of Congress Catalog-in-Publication Data
2015942861

Print ISBN 9781942672906
Ebook ISBN 9781942934257
Hardcover ISBN 9781942934264

Printed in the United States of America

Edited by Kelsey Cummings
Cover design by David Miles
Book design by Brooke Jorden

10 9 8 7 6 5 4 3 2 1

First Edition

INTENTIONAL
CONVERSATIONS

HOW TO RETHINK
EVERYDAY CONVERSATION
AND
TRANSFORM YOUR CAREER

KEN TUCKER

For my children, Kendra, Kristen, and Kenny; my granddaughter, Madelyn; my grandson, James Montgomery; my daughter-in-law, Lizzy; and my son-in-law, Tony:

YOU ARE MY IMPETUS FOR RETHINKING CONVERSATION.

ACKNOWLEDGMENTS

The input and wisdom of many important individuals are contained in this book. Bob Lacy, Jason Majesky, Jill Kamp Melton, Todd Hahn, Florence Hamm, Candice Whisenant, Jenny Rain, and Marianna Marko offered crucial feedback and clarifying suggestions on numerous occasions. My TAG partners, Joe Jurkowski, Jim Osterhaus, Kurt Andre, Mike Marino, and Kevin Ford, added the illustrative stories and examples that give life to the SECRET. Kelsey Cummings, my editor, insisted that each line and paragraph clearly communicate the lesson, logic, and power of an intentional conversation.

My wife, Judy, gave up many hours of personal and family time to discuss, interrogate, and fine-tune my embryonic ideas, unclear examples, incomplete concepts, and rambling stories.

Thousands of clients, others at TAG Consulting, and my friends have all contributed, through their conversations, many of the insights that are captured in this book. Thank you—*all of you*. Thank you for allowing me to be a student with you in the school of life as we continue to learn alongside each other how to get better and better at having intentional conversations.

FOREWORD

As is likely the case with most readers of *Intentional Conversations*, I don't remember my first conversation. In fact, I can barely remember several I had yesterday. The reason for that is simple— those easily forgettable conversations weren't intentional.

It doesn't have to be the case, however. I know I can improve because I've had a much better example, but like any worthwhile endeavor, it takes focus and effort.

As a not-so-young adult, I decided to change careers, leave the world of finance, and become a technology entrepreneur. I had no idea what I was doing. But I had an advantage that wasn't obvious at the time: my dad. He didn't know much about business or technology, either. But that didn't really matter. He is a gifted teacher, an effective communicator, and most importantly, knew how to ask the right question and follow it up with an intentional conversation. He combined that with an unwavering faith in his students' ability to solve their own problems if they ask and answer the right questions.

Recalling those memorable conversations with my dad wasn't difficult, even years later, not because I can remember the specific problem or question, but because I remember the feeling I usually left with. I felt encouraged to relax artificial, self-imposed constraints; empowered to take action; capable—I could do it; and supported—we were in it together.

Ken Tucker's *Intentional Conversations* is a fresh and positive reminder of the power of going beyond "shooting the breeze" and using conversation to get to the heart of work and life—learning what's in other people's hearts. So go ahead, ask a question, and start a conversation. One of my favorite intentional conversation starters is, "Are we missing anything?" I'm always amazed at what I learn.

JEFFREY S. HUSSEY
Advisor, Fluid Capital, LLC and NetBooks, Inc.
Co-Founder and former CEO, F5 Networks

CONTENTS

CHAPTER ONE

THINK, TALK, GROW

What is a significant "first" that you have had? What stands out for you? There are many significant "first" events that we experience as we are growing up. Some of them we remember with a sense of nostalgia. Others we recall with a smile. Still others we try not to remember. Some remain in our minds more clearly than others, like my first day of kindergarten, for example. I remember that day quite well. It started with my father dropping me off and placing me in the care of Ms. Thompson at the church-school around the corner from our house. As Ms. Thompson, my teacher, was busy receiving other students, I decided that I did not want to be at school. So I quietly left the school and proceeded toward home. But I knew better than to go home, so I hid between the neighbor's fence and my house. With my five-year-old brain, I thought I had my plan all figured out. Of course, I didn't; I was hiding in plain sight of the neighbor. The neighbor, Mrs. Taylor, called my father and told him where to find me. This "first" event, as you can imagine, was a painful one for me.

There are other "firsts" outside of the school realm that we remember as well. There is our first sweetheart, our first kiss, our first love. There is also our first bank account, first car, and first mortgage. For some of us, there is the birth of our first child, the first child off to college, the first child getting married, and the first grandchild. All of these "firsts" signal a stage of development, a level of growth. There is, however, one very significant "first" that happens that all of us experience, but few of us remember.

We all have a "first" conversation.

There is that specific day and time, that moment, that first instance when, as a child, we put together the thoughts, ideas, or information that launch us into a conversation with another person. It is a monumental event that few people, if any, remember at all. When was your first conversation? What was it about? Who was it with? What was the outcome? Sadly, like me, you probably cannot recall that momentous first conversation. It happened, you know it did, and it does not matter whether the conversation showed your brilliance, levity, innocence, simplicity, or hilarity— it is lost and gone forever.

Just think about it: for each of us, there was a time when conversation was a brand-new behavior. It may have been decades ago when, as a novice at conversation, you began logging your first few minutes of dialogue with another person. Since then, you have engaged in hundreds of thousands of conversations. By now, you are a veteran at all types of conversations. At this point in your life, you have had conversations that worked for you and ones that worked against you. You have had conversations that brought you joy and ones that caused you pain. You have had conversations that have changed your life or changed the lives of others. The fact is, once you had that initial conversation,

conversation became an integral part of every important event in your life. That is why I believe that conversation is something that we ought to think about far more often than we do.

Think about conversation—that is the first purpose of this book. As you read, think about what happens to you, through you, and between you and others because of conversation.

Rethink everyday conversation—that is the second purpose of this book. By the end of this book, you will recognize and realize the power conversation has to transform your career and relationships. Conversation sets us apart from all other animals. The use of spoken words to exchange ideas, thoughts, and information is a uniquely human ability. That is not to say animals do not communicate. They do. For instance, they use sound, body language, reaction, and a variety of other means to communicate alarm. Science has shown that all animals communicate. But humans alone have the capacity to have a conversation—to think and put those thoughts into words.

Conversation is so natural to us; we do it all the time without much thought—like when we pass someone in the hallway and exchange brief greetings then quickly forget that we ever had such an exchange. The exchange of ideas, thoughts, and information between people is an occasion that provides crucial and powerful opportunities that are often overlooked and undervalued.

Columnist Don Cote wrote an article in the *Las Vegas Informer* about a conversation that took place in 1908.[1] This conversation between Andrew Carnegie and Napoleon Hill lasted three days and changed (and still is changing) the lives of millions of people all around the world. At the end of the third day, Carnegie said to Hill, "Napoleon, I want to offer you a job. The job will take you twenty years to complete, and I'm not going to pay you."

Napoleon replied, "Not only will I take the job, Mr. Carnegie, you can count on me to complete it."

Carnegie responded, "I like the way you answered that. You have the job."

Carnegie continued on, "Here's the problem, Napoleon: people in this country are working too hard making a living and they have no time to figure out how to create a life. Men like myself know how to make lots of money. If you will interview the men I introduce you to the way you have interviewed me, you will discover "The Secret" and uncover our philosophy. You can then publish this philosophy and make it available to the common man."

Over a twenty-year period, Napoleon Hill did as Andrew Carnegie suggested and, as a result, published the book *Think and Grow Rich*[2]. To this day, no one has compiled a more comprehensive body of empirical research on the topic of how to become successful. The book is still a bestseller, has sold hundreds of millions of copies all around the world, and has been translated into over one hundred languages.

All as a result of one conversation.

WHAT WE SAY IN CONVERSATION MATTERS. THROUGH CONVERSATION, PEOPLE DECIDE WHETHER THEY LIKE US OR NOT . . .

People have conversations every day. Conversation is the universal means by which people engage one another. Wherever humans live, conversation is present. Using different sounds, words, signs, and symbols, humans conduct conversations in a variety of languages in every culture around the world. As compulsory as breathing, the human need to engage in conversation is undeniable.

What we say in conversation matters. Through conversation, people decide whether they like us or not, whether to follow us or not. Through conversation, we define who we are, who we want to become, and what our value is to others. Most importantly, it is through conversation that we get work done.

In the world of business, the amount of work that gets done is directly related to the frequency and quality of the conversations managers are having with their employees and the conversations employees are having with other employees. In negative instances, inappropriate conversations damage relationships, such as when words are used to intimidate, harass, or exclude employees from a group. In positive instances, conversation between employees reinforces the norms and expectations of the work culture, current goals, and the ways to achieve said goals. It is through conversations that casual and more personal relationships develop. And, through repeated conversation over time, trust, camaraderie, mutual respect, and team spirit can grow between employees.

The case is more complicated in conversations between managers and employees, however. Managers are largely the problem when employees decide to leave an organization. The Gallup Organization[3,4] reports that 70 percent of good employees leave due to limited or poor communication with their manager. The sad fact is that few managers are having relationship-building conversations with their employees. This creates a recurring and deteriorating cycle—managers do not have conversations with their employees, and, as a result, most employees do not know how to have a conversation with their managers.

A few years ago, the medical director of one of the foremost American medical teaching universities was asked the question,

"What are the conversations that your managers are having with their employees?" She was reluctant to answer—she was not at liberty to say, she finally admitted.

A CEO of a large hospital was asked the same question: What are the conversations that your managers are having with their employees? He said he did not know and did not think it important for him to know.

When the same question was asked of the CEO of a large group of companies valued in the billions of dollars, he demurred. He felt the question seemed too personal a subject for his style of leadership.

And when the question was posed to the CEO of a small construction firm, she responded that she did not know, but she imagined that the superintendents surely were talking to their workers on site.

When the dean of a four-year college was asked the same question—What are the conversations that your managers are having with their employees?—she responded there was no need to talk with the faculty because faculty and administration were separate departments. It was simply not something that ranked high on her list of leadership responsibilities.

As a consultant at TAG Consulting, much of my time is spent working with the chief decision makers of Fortune 500 companies; government agencies; healthcare, education, finance, and construction companies; and new business start-ups—both in the United States and across the globe—to identify strategic personnel changes and redesign or select new teams. A key process for us at TAG Consulting is seeking out what conversations managers are having with employees at the start of every consulting engagement as a way to gauge the manager's effectiveness. We are keenly aware of just how conversation impacts organizational and relationship goals.

John Gottman, a renowned psychologist and marriage therapist, has identified the impact conversation can have upon relationship longevity.[5] Building on twenty years of research, he has developed a way to predict which couples will remain married and which ones are likely to divorce. He makes this prediction based upon what he has found to be a reliable source of data—the couples' conversations. In 1991, Gottman designed a study with seven hundred newlywed couples. The couples were placed in a room and told to freely talk about any subject of their choosing. Gottman and his colleagues listened to each of the couples for five minutes and, based upon data gathered during the brief chat, predicted which couples would remain married. In 2001, Gottman's prediction of which couples would still be married, based on simply observing their conversations ten years earlier, turned out to be an astonishing 95 percent accurate. This amazing and accurate prediction, based upon the number of positive versus negative comments during a couple's conversation, is not only a reliable predictor of marital outcomes, but also points toward how conversation impacts other relationships as well, especially, in our experience, the ones found in business.

Conversation is, quite simply, the key to a strong business relationship, whether it be the relationship between business and customer, internal relationships among employees within the company, or the relationship between manager and employee.

Heather Wern, Director of Food Services in a busy hospital cafeteria, had one such conversation. In her case, she got more than just work done.

"A few months after I took over as the Director of Food

Services," Heather told me, "one of my top-performing kitchen workers stopped me. Early on, I had recognized that this particular employee appeared to have the potential to take on more responsibility than she had been given up to that point by her previous directors. So, I gradually started giving her various opportunities in order to assess where was the best fit for her. I was pleased when, in each instance, she shone. In fact, it seemed that with each new task I assigned her, she did the new task better than the one before. I was very pleased with her. So, when she stopped me and said, 'Thank you, Miss Heather, for helping me,' I immediately replied, 'No, thank you. Thank *you* for being so very good at your job.'"[6]

Heather's reply wasn't what the staff worker had expected—nor was the staff worker's reaction what Heather thought it would be. Instead of a pleased smile, the woman broke down in tears, sobbing, body-shaking tears.

"I pulled her quickly into the office there at the back of the kitchen," Heather recalls. "Then she told me her story, and tears flowed freely from my eyes, too. This kitchen worker of many years told me how just prior to my coming to work in the cafeteria, she had concluded that life was not worth living anymore. She had made up her mind to end her life. She had been busy putting things in order and making plans for her suicide. However, once I started calling upon her at work, she began to reconsider. She began to wonder if maybe there was some reason to live after all.

"'I just want to thank you for saving my life,' she said to me. 'Miss Heather, you just don't know how much you mean to me.'"

Conversations, though not as life-saving as this one, happen daily in the workplace. And, as in this example, managers and employees impact each other as they talk. What impact are you having upon the people you work with through your conversations? What results are you getting? How are you branding yourself? What mental image of you do people get from your conversation? How are you impacting your career through conversation?

Creating a reason for conversation is the one purpose of the Gallup Organization's multi-million-dollar national and global employee opinion survey. When administered within an organization, Gallup's Q12© solicits a response to such statements as "I have a best friend at work" and "At work, my opinions count." These unusual and, at times, seemingly intrusive survey items provide a reason for managers and their employees to have a conversation. Such was the case a few years ago when I was a Gallup consultant working with Toyota USA to coach several of their executives. One day, while I was on a coaching call with a regional sales manager, he told me the story about how his career had been painfully and revealingly impacted a year earlier:

> My scores [as a manager] on the Q12 were mediocre, with an overall score of 2.75 on a 5-point scale, but what really bothers me is the 1.20 score on the question, *My supervisor or someone at work cares about me as a person.* I felt compelled to find out what was driving that low score. So, I approached my assistant and expressed my disappointment with the results and asked her if she had any ideas about what may be negatively impacting team morale. She said she did not know but would ask around. She did and came back to me a few days later. "You are the problem," she told me. "Your behavior." I was stunned and insulted. I felt I had always been respectful and cordial with my employees. She agreed.

Then she told me it was not what I had done, but what I had failed to do.

"They call you Crickets. Yes, Crickets, like when it is so quiet you can hear the sound of crickets. You don't talk to them," she said quietly. "Just talk to them," she suggested. Again, I was stunned and a bit indignant. "That's it, talk to them?" "Yes," she said, "every morning you walk past your entire staff sitting at their desks without saying a word to anyone. Then, at lunchtime, you repeat it all over again. The only time you speak to them is when you have a request or some job-related subject to discuss." That conversation with my assistant changed my career and, in ways, changed my life. You see, a few days after that jarring conversation, I decided to change. I did not want to be Crickets. I am a list-maker; anything that I put on my list for the day gets done. So, every day now I write down on my list GET WATER, twice. Once in the morning and once in the afternoon as I leave my office to get water to drink, I stop and talk with an employee, and on the way back I stop and speak with another employee.

> WHEN CONVERSATION IS HEALTHY IN THE WORKPLACE, IT BRINGS IMPROVED RESULTS.

The results over the last twelve months have been remarkable. My decisions about the team and our work are far more informed, I know almost immediately when an employee finds a new way to solve a work-related problem—where in the past I would have never been included in the shoptalk that happens spontaneously. I know it is because of those few minutes of conversation that our Q12 scores are in the seventy-fifth percentile, and all of the questions are above 4.0! I have never been more excited about my work.

As seen in this example, we generally find that team cohesion and increased productivity are directly connected to the frequency of the conversations that are occurring within a team. When conversation is healthy in the workplace, it brings improved results. The opposite is also true. When conversation is limited or absent in the workplace, it leads to selective sharing and the stifling of information, which in turn can lead to disaster. Such was the case for one team on the morning of January 28, 1986.

Roger Boisjoly, a Morton-Thiokol engineer, describes an atmosphere in which conversation was limited or nonexistent between the Morton-Thiokol engineers and NASA decision makers leading up to the fateful launch of the *Challenger* space shuttle.[7] He wrote that the situation was one in which "intense intimidation was directed at the engineers." As a result, engineers and employees in general were afraid to have conversations in which they could freely express opinions. In this environment, information was neither free-flowing nor spontaneously shared. This coldness within the workplace was matched by the low temperatures outside on the launch pad. The night before the launch, the outside temperature fell to 18°F, and, on the morning of the launch, the temperature was only 36°F. While some engineers believed that the boosters would still be able to function safely under these conditions, many were very worried that the temperature would cause a failure.

But remember, Morton-Thiokol engineers did not feel safe

enough to have a conversation to convey their true concerns. They felt the decision makers were not likely to accommodate such a conversation. Six months before the space shuttle Challenger ultimately exploded over Florida on January 28, 1986, Roger Boisjoly had tried to engage in a conversation concerning the safety of the O-rings and seals by sending a memo to his supervisors at Morton-Thiokol. In that memo, he warned that if the weather was too cold, seals connecting sections of the shuttle's huge rocket boosters could malfunction. His concern was subsequently ignored by NASA. The night before the *Challenger*'s liftoff, when the temperature dipped below freezing, Mr. Boisjoly and other engineers did ask that the flight be postponed. Their bosses, not open to conversation as a regular and valued part of the workplace, missed an opportunity to discuss fully the risks the engineers were seeing pertaining to the launch. Seven crew members lost their lives that day—people who may yet be alive if the environment was such that that one meaningful conversation could have taken place between managers and employees.

Of course, not all conversations are life-changing or world-stopping events. However, it is through conversation that the important and pivotal lessons, relationships, events, and decisions in your life have occurred or are likely to occur.

Are there important, even critical, instances where, because of you, a conversation is not happening? Consider how important having a conversation could be to you, your career, your well-being, and that of others. Are there conversations your employees and managers need to be having?

Most people do not spend enough time thinking about conversation in this way. Maybe you are among the few who do. In any case, this book, *Intentional Conversations: How to Rethink*

Everyday Conversation and Transform Your Career, will teach you how to use conversation to improve your success at work and in your daily life.

ENDNOTES:

1. Cote, Don. "A Conversation That Changed the World." *Las Vegas Informer.* September 14, 2013. lasvegas.informermg.com/2013/09/14/a-conversation-that-changed-the-world-2/.

2. Hill, Napoleon. *Think and Grow Rich.* Tarcher, 2005.

3. Sahadi, Jeanne. "Signs you have a great job . . . or not." CNN Money. May 31, 2006. money.cnn.com/2006/05/31/commentary/everyday/sahadi/.

4. Beck, Randall, and Jim Harter. "Why Great Managers Are So Rare." *Gallup Business Journal.* March 25, 2014. www.gallup.com/businessjournal/167975/why-great-managers-rare.aspx.

5. Gottman, John M., and Joan DeClaire. *The Relationship Cure: A 5 Step Guide to Strengthening Your Marriage, Family, and Friendships.* Three Rivers Press, 2002.

6. Tucker, Ken. *Are you Fascinated?: The Four People You Need to Succeed.* Dailey Swann Publishing, 2009.

7. Martin, Douglas. "Roger Boisjoly, 73, Dies; Warned of Shuttle Danger." *The New York Times.* February 3, 2012. www.nytimes.com/2012/02/04/us/roger-boisjoly-73-dies-warned-of-shuttle-danger.html?_r=0.

CHAPTER TWO

FOOT IN MOUTH—OUCH!

Conversation is likely how you started your day. It may have occurred in the form of a half-asleep, half-awake, "How did you sleep?" exchange with your spouse, or a good morning greeting with a next-door neighbor, or casual banter at the checkout counter, or small talk with your carpool partner or a coworker. You will have many more conversations throughout the day. By the end of the day, you will have spoken thousands of words, uttered hundreds of sentences, and have had dozens of conversations. To what end? What will you have accomplished for all the effort and energy spent in conversation? Suppose this was how your effectiveness at work was being measured—by the number of conversations compared to the results achieved through them. Do you have any idea what your conversation outcome at work is like? Whether you realize it or not, your conversation outcome *is* being measured. In practical and indelible ways, the results that flow out of everyday conversation are measured, as was the case for a flight attendant and a friend of mine.

My friend was sitting in the crowded waiting area of Washington Dulles International Airport, about to take his third trip in four days and feeling quite burnt out. To the outside observer, he looked the part of a successful professional: business suit, well polished shoes, and power tie. But despite the appearance, he was not feeling very successful. He told me he had been sitting there thinking, "Why am I here at six in the morning, having spent the last three nights in one hotel after the other, enduring the ramblings of my overly nervous, over-caffeinated, cell-phone-babbling colleague, waiting to get on yet another flight to go see yet another client?"

Looking back on that moment, he could see how he was suffering from "stinking thinking," sabotaging himself before the day had even begun. His mental anguish grew as he tuned out his colleague's noisy banter to focus once again on the core of his questions. "Why am I subjecting myself to the hardships, the annoyances, and the dangers of contemporary travel? Is it for the money and prestige that accompany a successful career? Is it the lifestyle my labors support for myself and my family? Or do I have a nobler, more altruistic motivation?" These are weighty questions at any time, but at 6:15 a.m., they are gargantuan. Settling into his questions, he asked himself one more time: "Why do I do this job?"

At that moment, his flight was announced, and he and his eager colleague boarded the plane. As the plane reached cruising altitude, the flight attendants began the in-flight service, and my friend anxiously awaited his first cup of coffee. Sometime later, as the flight progressed, he was still in somewhat of a foul mood when it occurred to him that somehow everyone else around him had been served and he had not. He stopped the attendant as she passed by and brought his dire craving for coffee to her attention. She assured him that he would be taken care of immediately. Satisfied that coffee was on the way, he returned to his mental fuming about work and became lost again in thought.

Then much later, to his dismay, he realized that he had not yet, as promised, been served his coffee. Being already in a "poor me" state of mind, he did not take long to escalate to the next level—he was infuriated. He demanded to speak with the person in charge. When the purser (the supervisor of the flight attendants) came to him, he informed her in firm words that he would be filing a complaint about the poor service he had received from her and her colleagues. She listened quietly until he took a break from his ranting. Then, she quietly informed him that the flight attendant who was assigned to serve his area, a longtime professional named Wendy, had been particularly impressed with his demeanor and greeting as he boarded the plane.

He recounted to me that he had only used his "Good-morning-how-are-you-today?" greeting when he boarded, as he was having a miserable morning. Notwithstanding his lackluster greeting, the flight attendant in question had requested to be the one to serve him, according to the purser, because she felt, "He is a Jesse Jackson type. I know he is a preacher or something like that, and I just want to sit and chat with him during my break."

"She asked us to let her serve you," the purser said. "She is preparing to bring your coffee and one of our special treats. You will enjoy her. She has an album of pictures spanning her multi-decade career as a flight attendant, including pictures with Queen Elizabeth that she thought you would find interesting. This is normal for her. She usually finds someone to chat with on long flights during her break."

My friend was flabbergasted, embarrassed, and sorely disappointed in his own behavior. He stammered an apology to the purser for his behavior and begged her to ask Wendy to please come and share her story with him.

My friend got a rare second chance. Wendy—a soft-spoken, elegant, and humble lady—accepted his invitation and apology and expressed her own regret for not having communicated her intent more clearly. Wendy sat and shared her very interesting and eventful forty-year career with him for most of the flight.

My friend, with a smile, told me how they, at the end of the flight, exchanged e-mails and departed with a warm hug. He said repeatedly as he was sharing this story that he wished he could do it all over again and take back the angry words he had uttered, as the delightful outcome had come about only due to the purser's carefully considered conversation with him about her employee.

Wendy, the flight attendant, likewise could benefit from a redo. Had she told my friend earlier that she was planning to bring him a special treat, it would have allayed his concerns about having been overlooked or left out. Here is the moral of this story: all parties in this example are paid conversation professionals—yet these two experts failed.

My friend is a business consultant whose job success is measured by his ability to use conversation to coach executives daily. He had failed. Wendy's job requires her to be able to use conversation to assure, comfort, and inform a diverse audience of hundreds of travelers several times a day. She too had faltered. For both of them, their conversation outcome hit a low that day until the purser reset the conversation.

Everyone—manager, employee, you, and I—can benefit from some perspective and insight that will help us become more intentional in our conversations. That is why the principles in this book is so important for you to absorb. Conversation produces outcomes every time. We must not forget this.

Conversation is defined in the dictionary as the spoken exchange of thoughts, ideas, or information between people.[1] In this context, conversation involves your voice, your hands (for the hearing impaired), your words, your thoughts, and your ideas, and it involves the same things from the person with whom you are in conversation. Notice that this definition speaks only about the exchange and does not stipulate the results that come from the exchange. That is because simple conversation is just about people talking. Managers talk. Employees talk. However, a different kind of conversation, an *intentional conversation*, is required in the workplace if individuals and organizations are to succeed and avert failure.

> A DIFFERENT KIND OF CONVERSATION, AN INTENTIONAL CONVERSATION, IS REQUIRED IN THE WORKPLACE IF INDIVIDUALS AND ORGANIZATIONS ARE TO SUCCEED AND AVERT FAILURE.

My definition of an intentional conversation is "a spoken exchange of thoughts, ideas, and information *with collaborative and mutually-productive intent*." We *need* our conversation to be intentional. As business partners, managers, employees, parents, teachers, pastors, mentors, and simply citizens of a community, we want and need to be intentional, in a good way, with what we say. We also long to know that what we say is what we meant to say and what our listeners heard.

Unfortunately, lacking the right insight, attitude, tools, and skills for positive intentional dialogue, we often injure ourselves and others by saying the wrong thing or saying the right thing in the wrong way.

Everyday conversations are usually spontaneous. We throw thoughts and words together in an instant. When conversations happen, they often happen within the context of what is going on right there and then in our minds. We do not have a chance to edit and rewrite a conversation before it happens. Conversation happens on the spot, most times without prior warning or preparation. How often have you spoken words in conversation you wished you had not said? Words that came out wrong? Ideas that were incomplete? We have all said things we wish we could take back, rethink, or do over. What if this book equipped you to rethink and redo every significant conversation *before* it takes place? What if the proven strategies in this book could transform your career and improve your professional (and personal) relationships? Are you interested? If your answer is yes, then do this right now: write down or commit to memory the acronym SECRET. These six letters (S-E-C-R-E-T) will provide you with a mechanism by which you can become more intentional in each and every conversation you have.

The conversation in 1908 between Andrew Carnegie and Napoleon Hill could have easily gone quite differently if the ingredients of an intentional conversation had *not* been present. The story between Heather, the Director of Food Services, and her employee also could have turned out differently if Heather had not created the environment wherein an intentional conversation could take place. And maybe even the tragic results of the *Challenger* launch could have been different if the Morton-Thiokol managers, NASA decision makers, and their employees had worked within an environment intentionally designed to give voice to those who could challenge assumptions and where people felt they could be insistent and open in their conversation.

We have found that the quality and frequency of conversation makes an important difference in the outcomes produced by managers, employees, and organizations. This past year alone, TAG Consulting studied and evaluated almost seven hundred individual manager-to-employee conversations. We have used *The Engagement Guide©*, our manager and employee interview tool, over the last ten years to foster intentional conversation in the business setting.[2] We have also studied the conversations of hundreds of the highest-performing employees across various industries through our idMatch© Selection Process.[3] From all this data we have collected over the years, we have learned that effective managers create an environment where they and their employees are able to, and are likely to, have intentional conversations.

An intentional conversation requires six actions to be taken by those who are in dialogue. These six actions, which we will identify and discuss fully in later chapters, are found in the acronym SECRET, which hopefully you wrote down and will remember. For now, here is a little about what we know about the impact of SECRET. We know that when SECRET is practiced, employees, careers, and organizations are positively impacted. We know that when SECRET is used by managers, they make more informed decisions and their teams are more productive. We know that when SECRET is

> AN INTENTIONAL CONVERSATION REQUIRES SIX ACTIONS TO BE TAKEN BY THOSE WHO ARE IN DIALOGUE.

taught and embraced by teams, collaboration and the team's ability to solve problems increase.

Why does SECRET work? SECRET works because it *resets the social reality* that exists between people—like, for example, how the purser reset the situation between Wendy the flight attendant and my friend. Every time we engage in conversation, we are either confirming or creating a social reality between the two parties. Whether it is our spouse, sibling, supervisor, or whomever, the ideas, thoughts, and information shared in a conversation are based upon the social reality that exists. If we are talking about what is for dinner tonight, it is more likely to be a conversation between us and our spouse rather than one with our boss. However, according to the relationship that exists, we may just as readily ask our boss questions such as, "How are you feeling today?" or "What do you need help with?" Our conversation is tempered by the social reality that exists at the moment.

"How we address people," says Norman Markel, PhD, Professor Emeritus at the University of Florida, "what we self-disclose, where we sit, how we make eye contact, and where and when we touch are the five vital signs of conversation, communicating how we feel about each other. And, most important from the standpoint of Conversation Psychology, no matter what we are talking about in a conversation, we are always broadcasting our attitudes and emotions about friendship and social status."[4] It is in this way, without even realizing it, that managers and employees send messages that prevent or impede important conversations from happening.

The SECRET process promotes conversation. It resets the social status that exists between manager and employee. Once managers and employees practice SECRET, managers are no longer seen as walking around with loaded guns, as it were. The "loaded gun" analogy represents the authority the manager has due to his or her position. As it stands, managers are generally viewed as walking around armed with power over employees. In many cases, the manager has the power to derail careers and lives. The manager, just by position, can be feared and often not trusted. Why? Because they have authority that employees do not have. Too often in conversation with a manager, this "loaded gun" is flashed intimidatingly for all to see. Employees learn to guard what they say, much like in the case with NASA and the engineers. This "loaded gun" syndrome is, unfortunately, very present in many organizations today. Therefore, in order to apply SECRET, managers and employees must first upgrade their thinking from that of merely having *conversation* to that of having *intentional conversation*.

Recall that the dictionary defines conversation as the spoken exchange of thoughts, ideas, and information. In contrast, an intentional conversation is the spoken exchange of thoughts, ideas, and information *with collaborative and mutually productive intent*. When managers and employees practice intentional conversations, they turn their attention toward measuring and improving their conversation outcome. Simply put, managers and employees become more intent upon using conversation in a way that produces mutually rewarding results. SECRET provides the framework and strategy by which manager and employee, through intentional conversations, transform their careers and relationships.

Throughout this book, I will provide exercises so that you can apply what I am teaching you to your personal experiences. These sections are called "SECRET Opportunities."

SECRET OPPORTUNITY #1

Remember, SECRET works because it *resets the social reality*, the social status, that exists between people. When we engage in conversation, we confirm or create a social reality between us and the other party based on how we choose to interact with that person and what we choose to say. **Here is a real life example of a "social status" situation:**

This conversation was between one of our consultants and John S. earlier this year: The consultant arrived at the regularly scheduled meeting and, as he sat down, he noticed a crisp one hundred dollar bill on the table. He turned to John and asked what the bill was for, pointing at the money. John walked over from where he was standing at his elevated draftsman desk, picked up the hundred dollars, and put it away in his wallet, saying, "Oh yeah, I put this there for you, providing you came on time, and as I predicted, you were late again—about three minutes too late to collect the money."

In this setting, John S. establishes his "one up" position by showing that he could afford to give away a hundred dollars. He also placed the consultant in a "one down" position by reminding him that he was late (by three minutes, according to his watch) again.

IN THE SPACE BELOW, IN AS MUCH DETAIL AS YOU CAN,
RECOUNT AN ACTUAL CONVERSATION YOU HAD IN WHICH
SOCIAL STATUS WAS EVIDENT:

ENDNOTES:

1. *Dictionary.com.* "conversation." www.dictionary.reference.com/browse/conversation?s=t.

2. TAG Consulting. "The Engagement Guide©."

3. TAG Consulting. "idMatch© Selection Process."

4. Markel, Norman. "Applied Conversation Psychology." *Conversation Psychology.* May, 2012. www.psychologyofconversation.com/default.html.

CHAPTER THREE

THE *S* IN SECRET

SUSPEND STATUS: to communicate in a way that values and esteems the other person as equal to or higher than yourself.

Conversation at times can be more revealing than we intend or expect, like when one person admits to the other, "I have a lover." How would you react if you were the person hearing those words? What would you be silently saying to yourself? What if those words were said to you in confidence by a Benedictine monk? Laurel Robbins, award-winning travel blogger and world traveler, had that experience. She writes:

> You know your conversation with a Benedictine monk is going to be interesting when one of the first things he says is "I have a lover . . ." his eyes dancing with mischief. My eyes grow wide in anticipation as Brother Ignatius

pauses dramatically. "... God," he says laughing. I'm not a religious person, but I was fascinated and intrigued by my conversation with Brother Ignatius. The conversation was peppered with humor and spirituality. I didn't want it to end and I could have talked to him for hours.

I don't plan on becoming a monk, or even going to church more often, if I'm being completely honest—sorry to disappoint you, Brother Ignatius (but, then again, you wouldn't be disappointed because monks aren't supposed to have wants, right?)—but I left our conversation full of gratitude. Grateful that Brother Ignatius opened my mind and made me think in a different way. Grateful to challenge some of my ideas about . . . entertainment. Thankful that he cleared up some of the misconceptions I had about monks and about life in a monastery, which I had previously imagined to be rather dull. So thank you, Brother Ignatius; your time with me was not wasted, and I continue to reflect upon our conversation.[1]

There is a very important lesson we can learn about the SECRET process from this conversation. First, remember that, when we practice SECRET, we are resetting our social reality— we level the ground between us and the other person. Notice how position, affluence, authority, rank, and title between the blogger and the monk are absent from the interaction. The monk did not come across as "holier than thou" or sanctimonious. He did not take a "one up" position. Instead, he made himself vulnerable with his well-placed admission, "I have a lover." He was determined to connect with Laurel. To do this, he placed himself in a "one down" position first, and took the risk of giving Laurel the "one up" position.

Dr. James Osterhaus, in his book *Questions Couples Ask Behind Closed Doors*, explains that a healthy relationship is one in which both parties agree to take turns being "one up" and "one down."[2] This type of surrender is especially needed in a manager-to-employee relationship where, as we noted earlier, a manager is most often placed in the "one up" position with a "loaded gun." Managers have, by title and function, a specific and recognized status in the workplace—they are the boss. Too many managers are either oblivious or obstinate when it comes to how their conversation broadcasts their status in a negative way. Effective managers, on the other hand, care about how their employees experience the status of their title, and they do as the monk did,

EFFECTIVE MANAGERS CARE ABOUT HOW THEIR EMPLOYEES EXPERIENCE THEM.

they *suspend* status. *Suspend* is the first word and the first action step in SECRET. To "suspend status" means to understand and own the status you have, but to choose to behave and communicate in a way that values and esteems the other person as equal to or higher than yourself. So what does suspending status look like?

Carolyn Crawford became famous when she witnessed firsthand what it looks and feels like to suspend status. In her book *Fabled Service*, Betsy Sanders writes about Carolyn's memorable day at the local Nordstrom department store in her hometown.[3] As Carolyn was walking into Nordstrom, her attention was caught by the person walking ahead of her into the store—a bag lady clad in torn, filthy clothes. Convinced that the woman would be turned away by the security personnel, she decided to follow the bag lady through the store with the intent of intervening with security and softening the blow to the woman's dignity when she was asked to leave. To Carolyn's relief and surprise, no one prevented the woman's journey to the Special Occasions Department.

There, surrounded by the elegant ambiance of holiday decorations and music from a stringed quintet, Carolyn watched within hearing distance as a conversation ensued between the bag lady and a well-dressed saleswoman. Carolyn became transfixed with the scene that unfolded before her. She watched with awe as time and again, with friendly and attentive service, the saleswoman brought item after item for the unlikely customer to try on. Carolyn watched with interest as the conversation and comfort grew between the two women. They chatted and laughed freely together. At times they agreed on the look and sometimes they disagreed. After a while, when the lady had tried on all the fine dresses, handbags, and matching accessories she and the saleswoman had selected, she thanked the saleswoman for her time and left without purchasing a single item.

After watching the woman leave, Carolyn approached the saleswoman and asked her, "Why did you do that?"

Not understanding the question, the saleswoman asked, "Sorry, I do not understand, but do what?"

"Why did you take so much time with that lady just now who probably has no means to afford your products?"

The saleswoman answered, "This is what we are here for: to serve and to be kind."

The next Sunday at Bel Air Presbyterian Church in Los Angeles, as the Reverend Carolyn Crawford stood in the pulpit, the congregation was abuzz with excitement and anticipation in regards to her sermon title: *The Gospel According to Nordstrom.*

Great story, right? Indeed. Reverend Carolyn's sermon and

the story about the saleswoman became national news. The *New York Times* carried the story (August 27, 1989), as did several television stations.[4] But why is this story important to us in this book? What Reverend Carolyn witnessed is what we call an intentional conversation—words spoken with a collaborative and mutually productive intent. The saleswoman created the environment for an intentional conversation by first leveling the social ground between her and the customer—by suspending status. Although the woman appeared to be unable to afford any of the clothes in the store, the saleswoman ignored any indicator of the bag lady's status and treated her with the esteem and value that people want and deserve.

Similar stories and the same type of affirming, empowering impact are likely to occur when managers suspend status. Jim, manager at St. Paul Insurance Company in St. Paul, Minnesota, was in charge of 1,400 employees in the claims department. He tells the story of an employee that had been given the nickname "Ms. Brash" by the supervisors in the department. She earned her nickname, he explained, and lived up to it by being obnoxious and unruly. He only knew of her because her misbehavior had escalated to the point where he was called upon to intervene. The meeting didn't seem to bode well for her. Jim asked her what he could do to help her in this situation. Her reply both shocked and informed him. Ms. Brash, in her indomitable way, responded to his question with, "You can give me my vacation and my severance pay."

Now most managers reading this (and most consultants) would have advised Jim to accept her offer on the spot. But Jim did not do that, because in that moment it became clear to him how he could possibly help her. He decided that he would put to the test some of the strategies my fellow TAG consultants and I were teaching him and his managers. These strategies are all part of the SECRET I am revealing in this book. Instead of accepting her offer to resign, Jim offered her the opportunity to help him with a project. Ms. Brash was surprised and a bit suspicious, Jim noted, but she relented and accepted his offer. What Jim did over the next six months illustrates perfectly how the SECRET of intentional conversation can help you rethink everyday conversations and transform your career and those of others.

First, Jim reset the social status inside his head. He repeated this mantra to himself every time he interacted with Ms. Brash: "How can I be her partner to help her discover just how good at her job she can be?" This started off as just a way for him to tolerate her obnoxiousness. It gradually became his commitment to her, and he found himself simply wanting to help her as a person.

Through his ongoing conversations with Ms. Brash, Jim discovered what tasks Ms. Brash actually did well. Then, based upon that information, he asked Ms. Brash to do those tasks to help him to do his own work. The increase in productivity, collegiality, and workplace engagement was nothing short of transformational for Ms. Brash, and also for Jim.

No longer was she an intolerable employee to him, but more and more he began seeing her as an equal partner, as she began working harder to get along with others. Such is the power of suspending status—it not only levels the ground between us, but also expands the opportunity for us to learn more about each other.

When managers learn how the status differential between them and their employees impacts their ability to be effective, and then use that heightened awareness to suspend status, they release themselves and their employees to engage freely in intentional conversations. The result in every instance, in my experience, is an increase in positive workplace outcomes.

Status always exists, both in the workplace and in daily life. Suspending status requires being aware of the moments when you have status. Like many managers, you may be the one with a loaded gun and not realize the negative impact it is having upon your conversation. You are likely to be the one with social status in a conversation when:

- The other person has recognized and accepted that they have made a mistake or taken action that has harmed you in some way.
- You have something that the other person needs or wants.
- The other person believes that you have information that can hurt, enrich, or impact him or her directly.
- You are perceived as having the power to continue or end a relationship.
- The other person is organizationally, relationally, or voluntarily under your authority.

Status is always present and, as you can see from the list above, potentially threatening. That is why managers and other people with status, perceived or otherwise, need to work hard to level the ground between them and the other person. It is how we use status in conversation that makes the difference in the results we achieve. Whether manager-to-employee, parent-to-child, spouse-to-spouse, or friend-to-friend, we can choose during every conversation how we use our status. Mark Zuckerberg, CEO of Facebook—well-known for positioning himself as equal to, and at times "one down," with his employees—chooses to suspend status. In her book *Lean In*, the chief operating officer of Facebook and author Sheryl Sandberg describes one such instance:

A few years ago, Mark Zuckerberg decided to learn Chinese. To practice, he spent time with a group of Facebook employees who were native speakers. One might think that Mark's limited language skills would have kept these conversations from being substantively useful. Instead, they gave him greater insight into what was going on in the company. For example, one of the women was trying to tell Mark something about her manager. Mark didn't understand, so he said, "Simpler, please." Then she spoke again, but he still didn't understand, so he had to ask her to simplify further. This happened a few more times. Eventually, she got frustrated and just blurted out, "My manager is bad." She was still speaking Chinese, but simply enough that Mark understood.[5]

Zuckerberg chose to suspend status and, as a result, received more value from the conversation than he anticipated. That is usually the case—employees will share the real issues and problems that are present in the workplace—if managers engage in conversation in a way that helps employees know that they are valued and respected.

> WHEN WE ESTEEM THE OTHER PERSON, WE GET BACK MORE FROM THE CONVERSATION THAN WE EVER COULD HAVE ANTICIPATED.

Employees, on the other hand, can actually help managers suspend status by empowering themselves. Employees empower themselves by exceeding expectations and helping others. By doing their work exceedingly well and helping coworkers, employees can change the way work gets done. Work, in this instance, gets done by collaborative effort, each person helping the other person succeed. This employee-empowerment results in a noticeable change for the manager, as the need to exercise managerial authority diminishes. As a result, managers can now engage with employees differently. The conversation changes—it becomes one of empowerment. When people are empowered and empower others, they begin to practice intentional conversation. When we suspend status in our conversations—that is, when we value and esteem the other person—we get more back from the conversation than we could ever have anticipated.

SECRET OPPORTUNITY #2

Identify a situation in which you might need to suspend status. How can you benefit from suspending the status? Is it your status or that of the other person that needs suspending?

Remember how position, affluence, authority, rank, and title between the blogger and the monk were absent from their interaction. Managers have, by title and function, a specific and recognized status in the workplace—they are the boss. Effective managers, though, care about how their employees experience the status of their title, and they do as the monk did, they *suspend* status. Once a manager and employee are on equal footing, there is room for intentional conversations to happen.

MAKE A LIST OF THE POSITIONS YOU HOLD IN YOUR DAILY LIFE AND AT WORK WHERE YOU HAVE STATUS. HOW IS YOUR CONVERSATION IN EACH INSTANCE BEING IMPACTED BY YOUR STATUS?

ENDNOTES:

1. Robbins, Laurel. "Conversations with a Benedict Monk in Norcia, Umbria." *Monkeys and Mountains Adventure Travel Blog.* June 19, 2012. www.monkeysandmountains.com/benedict-monk-umbria.

2. Osterhaus, James. *Questions Couples Ask Behind Closed Doors: How to Take Action on the Most Common Conflicts in Marriage.* Familius, 2014.

3. Sanders, Betsy. *Fabled Service: Ordinary Acts, Extraordinary Outcomes.* Amsterdam: Pfeiffer & Co., 1995.

4. Stevenson, Richard W. "Watch Out Macy's, Here Comes Nordstrom." *The New York Times.* August 26, 1989. www.nytimes.com/1989/08/27/magazine/watch-out-macy-s-here-comes-norstrom.html.

5. Sandberg, Sheryl, and Nell Scovell. *Lean In: Women, Work, and the Will to Lead.* New York: Knopf, 2013.

CHAPTER FOUR

THE FIRST *E* IN SECRET

EMPOWER EACH PERSON: to serve the other person during conversation in a way that validates you have his or her interests and well-being in mind.

C hange your conversation and it will change your world and, in particular, your career and your relationships—this would be a grandiose statement if it were not true. However, it *is* true; conversations have the power to change things, and according to researcher Judith Glaser, author of *Conversational Intelligence:*

> Positive conversations produce a chemical reaction, too. They spur the production of oxytocin, a feel-good hormone that elevates our ability to communicate, collaborate, and trust others by activating networks in our prefrontal cortex. This "chemistry of conversations" is why

it's so critical for all of us—especially managers—to be more mindful about our interactions.[1]

John Gottman, in the research we mentioned earlier, identified a "magic ratio" for the impact conversation has upon people. He found that when the couples he was observing used five times as many positive comments as negative in their conversations, Gottman could predict that those couples were likely to remain married after ten years. As you remember from chapter one, he was 95 percent correct. The takeaway from this research is clear: our conversation, negative or positive, impacts the outcomes we achieve. So, yes, change your conversation to change your life and the lives of others. Make conversation empowering. That is the progressive next action step in the SECRET process—for managers and employees to change their conversation by empowering each other. The second word and next step is *empower*— Empower each person. To empower a person, in this context, is to be intent on serving the other person in a way that validates you have their interests and well-being in mind.

CHANGE YOUR CONVERSATION, CHANGE YOUR LIFE.

In the last chapter, the monk, the saleswoman, and the manager demonstrated the first step—*suspend status.* There is a necessary sequence in the SECRET—whoever has status (perceived, formal, or relational) must yield that status first in order for the other person to feel safe enough to enter into an intentional conversation. Then, once on equal footing, both parties are more prepared to take the next step of empowering each other. This is a forward-moving process. This process itself is the difference—a mere conversation begins when someone exchanges words with another person. An *intentional conversation*, however, begins when a person feels comfortable enough to speak up and trust the other person with what he or she is really thinking. People are more likely to share concerns and innovative ideas freely when they feel empowered, when they feel validated and accepted. To get to this safe place where people willingly share thoughts and ideas, managers and employees will need to change their conversation, as the research below reveals.

Management researchers Kathleen Ryan and Daniel Oestreich discovered in their workplace development study that 70 percent of employees across a variety of industries and job types hesitated to speak up about problems at work or suggest possible improvements to their firm because they feared repercussions.[2] Their research reinforces how fear of retribution, which is oftentimes enforced by the "one-up," "loaded-gun" status of the manager, inhibits robust and helpful conversation. There is no sense of empowerment in these situations.

AN INTENTIONAL CONVERSATION IS PROGRESSIVE. EACH STEP LAYS THE FOUNDATION FOR THE ONE THAT FOLLOWS.

In another study, Cornell management professor James Detert found that only 51 percent of employees he studied said they felt safe speaking up most of the time.[3] Most employees are afraid to engage in meaningful conversations about work with their managers. These employees do not feel empowered enough to engage in work-related conversations. So what can be done to reverse this trend?

An intentional conversation is progressive—each step lays the foundation for the one that follows. The first step, *suspend status*, levels the social ground between manager and employee, entreating employees to start conversations with managers. This second step, *empower each person*, facilitates a new way of thinking that commits managers, employees, and peers to serving each other. A manager practicing this step will often do the unusual thing of serving the needs of the employee rather than expecting or demanding to be served.

"Serving others and practicing loving kindness is not the first image that comes to mind when we think about corporate executives or leaders of organizations," Lance Secretan writes in his book *Inspirational Leadership.*[4] He continues, "This may be because we train aggression into contemporary leaders. When Cornell University asked 250 business-school students what traits they thought made a great leader, they put being results-oriented at the top of their list, and 60 percent said they admired slash-and-burn downsizers like 'Chainsaw' Al Dunlap."

Our entire society has long valued and rewarded the harsh, self-made, rough-talking "John Wayne" type of manager in the workplace. The former CEO of American Airlines was often hailed as a hero of the airline industry. Inside his organization, he was quietly called "Fang" and "Darth Vader," the villain from the *Star Wars* movie series.[5] Likewise, Jack Welch, former CEO of GE, was voted four times as "most respected" by *Industry Week.*[6] Inside the company, *Fortune* magazine reported that he was always on the attack, criticizing, demeaning, ridiculing, and humiliating.[7] Yet he is celebrated as one of the heroes of industry. Somehow, in the recent past, we seem to have concluded in business that it does not matter how people feel about what we say to them. It's as if our society has given a special dispensation to corporate managers, giving them permission to be harsh, even cruel, without recourse just as long as the business succeeds. Thankfully, that thinking and those practices are changing. There is a clarion call today for managers to change the tenor of their conversation to one of service and empowerment.

Employees practicing the *empower each person* step likewise must rethink their own conversation in terms of serving, deciding instead to serve *alongside* their managers, rather than from beneath or reluctantly. This was the case for employees at Randolph Medical Center. Tommy, the CEO, was appalled to discover that, on an employee engagement survey, the majority of the center's employees reported that they felt either emotionally disconnected from their organization or frustrated at work. Our TAG consultants discovered that the employee-to-employee conversations demonstrated a high degree of apathy and disengagement. Employees were quick to deflect responsibility. Regularly, in conversations we observed, employees repeated, "It's not my job," and "They don't pay me enough to work that hard." For employees of this organization, this was simply "how it was at work."

Transcripts of employee conversations at this hospital showed that many employees described their work as either painful or disappointing. They had no expectations of connection, satisfaction, or fulfillment from their jobs. At the time of the survey, various other indicators confirmed how low morale was directly affecting performance. One place where the negative impact was clear and acute was the emergency department. This is how Tommy described the situation and the subsequent action he and his team took to turn it around:

> The leadership team was determined to put a stop to this demotivating and unresponsive situation. That spring, we began hiring nurses with a unique appetite for the challenge of the emergency department. Then, we tied

their performance to the metric of Left Prior to Medical Screening Exam, which at the time was 11.9 percent. That went down to 2.9 percent after three months. How did we do it? We didn't—the staff did.

This remarkable change in the ER led our consultants to look deeper into this hospital. What they discovered was that this turn around started first with a group of nurses who got together at lunch to discuss the survey results. Over time, as the lunches caught on, more and more employees joined the meeting. In an interview, one nurse said, "We were getting such a large amount of people at the lunches that there were hardly any chairs left for others who were not a part of the meeting. One day, a manager was annoyed by not being able to find a seat and in disgust yelled, 'You, you morale boosters are busting my morale by taking all the chairs!' We laughed, apologized, and gave him a chair. But the name stuck. That is where we got the formal name of our group from; we are the Morale Boosters."

And they were indeed boosting morale. What made the group so effective and, therefore, attractive to others, was its focus on empowering each member. Employees discussed their challenges, frustrations, and even their failures in an open but safe and empowering forum. The employees had created an environment in which they could feel safe and valued. This was now a place where employees knew that their peers cared about their concerns and would do anything they could to help them succeed. By the time the next survey came around twelve months later, this hospital was among the top 10 percent in employee attachment and performance out of two hundred hospitals.

From this story (and the conversation between Andrew Carnegie and Napoleon Hill in chapter one), we can glean three important essentials that must be present in order to effectively empower others. The first essential is *personal mission*.

Every person has a mission. When Carnegie, one of the richest and most successful men of that day, said to Hill, "Napoleon, I want to offer you a job. The job will take you twenty years to complete and I'm not going to pay you," Hill could have rejected the offer right away. He did not, however, because Hill had a personal mission that he shared with Carnegie—to impact the world.

The second essential of empowerment, what we call *heartitude*, was shared by both Andrew Carnegie and Napoleon Hill. They practiced the same kind of thinking that all who take the time to invest in an intentional conversation will have—heartitude. Heartitude is the sincere appetite to serve others. It cannot be forced or faked. When our conversation is seasoned with a desire to serve, people sense it. This paves the way for a deeper connection, which we will learn more about in the next chapter.

The third essential for empowerment is *confidence in others*. Carnegie put his confidence in Hill. By doing that, he affirmed and validated Hill's contribution. Empowering others requires believing in them. It requires staking your reputation upon what the other person says they will do.

We saw the same kind of confidence from Andrew Carnegie when Napoleon replied, "Not only will I take the job, Mr. Carnegie, you can count on me to complete it." Carnegie replied, "I like the way you answered that. You have the

WHEN OUR CONVERSATION IS SEASONED WITH A DESIRE TO SERVE, PEOPLE SENSE IT.

job!" There was emotion between these two men. Carnegie liked what Hill was saying, and Hill liked what Carnegie was offering.

Conversation is as much about emotion as it is about content. During conversation, we reciprocate emotion. We exchange feelings.

In the movie *Patch Adams*, starring the late Robin Williams, the dean of students is opening the new semester with his usual speech.[8] Patch and his new friends are listening with anticipation, some more rapt than others. The dean concludes emphatically with this statement: "The sad fact is human beings are not worthy of trust; it is human nature to lie, take shortcuts, lose your nerve, get tired, make mistakes. No rational patient would put trust in a human being, and we are not going to let him. It is our mission here to rigorously and ruthlessly train the humanity out of you and make you into something better. We are going to make doctors out of you!" At which time the audience of young eager minds erupts with applause—that is, all but Patch.

Patch has a different perspective. He actually believes that a greater focus on our humanity needs to be put back into medicine. Because of his belief, he invites his friend to help him with an experiment, which he proceeds to conduct on the street. The objective of his experiment, he tells his fellow student, is to get an emotional response from unsuspecting pedestrians by initiating a conversation with them with one word: "hello." In hilarious fashion, Patch proves his point as every stranger he approaches reacts, just as he hypothesized, with a positive emotion to his warm and hearty greeting. This scene from the movie is directly relevant to what we are teaching in this book: humans react to the emotion of a conversation.

> IN CONVERSATION, WE HEAR THE WORDS, BUT WE FEEL THE ATTITUDE.

In conversation, we hear the words, but we feel the attitude. It is the feeling we get from people in conversation that sticks with us more than the words. It is how we feel that brings us back to or keeps us away from conversation with a particular person.

This is the step, *empower each person*, that etches in the minds of a stranger or friend the good feeling that comes from us serving each other. Through this step, managers and employees begin to forge a new kind of reciprocal relationship, one that defies the classic but archaic practice of harsh management. During your conversation, you are attaching positive emotion to your name in the other person's mind. To do this, remember how the three essentials of empowerment are practiced in the examples we have discussed so far:

Personal mission: Patch Adams (not the character in the movie, but the real man) has a personal mission. Hunter Doherty "Patch" Adams is an American physician, social activist clown, and author. His personal mission is to provide free healthcare, so he founded the Gesundheit! Institute, a free community clinic, in 1971.[9] Each year, to generate interest and support for the clinic, he organizes a group of volunteers from around the world to travel to various countries, where they dress as clowns to bring humor to orphans, patients, and other people. Other people can see and feel your personal mission, or lack thereof.

Heartitude: The Morale Boosters changed the culture at Randolph Medical Center through the vehicle of serving others—they had heartitude. People respond positively in an environment in which your service proves that you value and care about them.

Confidence in others: Jim, the manager from St. Paul Company we wrote about in chapter three, was willing to risk his own reputation by investing in and trusting that Ms. Brash could and would change her behavior. When people know you trust them, they are most likely to give trust in return.

Conversation, in essence, is a forum in which people learn how to feel about each other. Every time we have a conversation, we scan through our emotions, attaching the ones that fit with how we feel about the person to that person. The next time we see that person, even if we forgot the content of the last conversation, we are more likely to remember the emotion we experienced during that conversation. The more conversations we have with a person, the more those feelings are reinforced or replaced. When we practice the second step, *empower each person*, we add positive emotion to the conversation. It is that emotion that becomes embedded in our minds. Judith Glasser writes, "Conversations carry meaning that become more embedded in the listener than the speaker. We connect to others through conversations." What does conversation with you feel like? What emotion is being attached to your name as a result of your conversations?

SECRET OPPORTUNITY #3

What is the most empowering thing you have done recently? Who benefited? How?

Remember that an intentional conversation is progressive:

1. *Suspending status* levels the social ground between manager and employee.
2. *Empowering each person* commits managers, employees, and peers to serving each other.

A manager practicing this second step will serve his or her employees rather than expecting or demanding to be served.

Employees likewise must decide instead to serve *alongside* their managers, rather than from beneath or reluctantly.

WHAT IS YOUR DEFINITION OF EMPOWERMENT? HOW DID ANDREW CARNEGIE EMPOWER NAPOLEON HILL?

ENDNOTES:

1. Glaser, Judith E. *Conversational Intelligence: How Great Leaders Build Trust and Get Extraordinary Results*. Bibliomotion, 2013.

2. Ryan, Kathleen D., and Daniel K. Oestreich. *Driving Fear Out of the Workplace: Creating the High-Trust, High-Performance Organization*. 2nd ed. Jossey-Bass, 1998.

3. Detert, James R., and Ethan R. Burris. "Managerial modes of influence and counterproductivity in organizations: A longitudinal business-unit-level investigation." *Journal of Applied Psychology* 92, no. 4 (July 2007): 993-1005.

4. Secretan, Lance H. K. *Inspirational Leadership: Destiny, Calling and Cause*. Toronto: Macmillan Canada, 1999.

5. "The Airline Mess." *Bloomberg Businessweek*. July 5, 1992. www.bloomberg.com/bw/stories/1992-07-05/the-airline-mess.

6. *Industry Week*. December 21, 2004.

7. *Fortune*. January 25, 1993.

8. Shadyac, Tom. *Patch Adams*. Videocassette. Universal Pictures, 1998.

9. The Gesundheit! Institute. www.patchadams.org

CHAPTER FIVE

THE *C* IN SECRET

CULTIVATE CONNECTION: to create an environment of mutual giving and receiving in order to forge a deeper relationship.

Conversation is a bridge. It automatically connects one person to the other. It does not matter if it is a momentary encounter or a longer event. Whenever we have a conversation, a connection is made between us and the other person.

A brief one-word exchange on the elevator creates a connection. "Hello," the person entering the elevator says to you. "Hi," you reply quietly. Connection is that quick and that automatic due to the sheer nature of conversation. Although the connection in this instance is short-lived and quickly discarded, for five seconds or so, you were joined in conversation with that person.

What I say to you and what you say to me connects us to each other through the act of speaking and hearing. An in-depth connection, on the other hand, is not automatic. Most of our conversations are indeed superficial and fleeting, sometimes just elevator chats. We have to *cultivate* our connection in order for the exchange to progress to the level of an intentional conversation. And for us to want to invest that effort there needs to be a reason for the conversation. The third word and subsequent step in SECRET is *cultivate*—cultivate connection. To *cultivate connection* is to invest the time, energy, and risk needed to create an environment of mutual giving and receiving in order to forge a deeper relationship.

Cultivating a connection is work for both parties. Where suspending status is work for a manager or anyone with status, and empowering each other is work for each individual, cultivating connection requires mutual effort on both the part of the manager and the employee. If any party missteps here, the exchange will remain a superficial conversation. But how do we cultivate connections deep enough that we can have intentional conversations? We start by understanding how cultivation works. To understand how managers and employees can cultivate enough depth of connection to have intentional conversations, we need to take a short break from our manager/employee focus to look at Cultivation Theory.

Cultivation Theory, a social theory identified by George Gerbner and Larry Gross, examines the long-term effects of television.[1] The primary proposition of Cultivation Theory states that the more time people spend living in the television world, the more likely they are to believe the social reality portrayed on television. Simply put, Cultivation Theory proposes that the more we are exposed over the long term to the norms, behaviors, values, and standards we see on television, the more prone we are to take those as our reality. It says that people gradually come to accept the view of the world portrayed on TV, in particular, as a true representation of reality and adapt their hopes, fears, and understandings accordingly.

The more people view TV, the more their ideas correspond with the television view. It is gradual, cumulative, and indelible. In this way, Cultivation Theory helps us to understand the difficulty managers and employees face when it comes to cultivating connection. Just as constant immersion into the TV world forms reality, so does the historical and pervasive experience of how managers and employees are "supposed" to interact form the reality for those in the workplace. The prevalent image of the relationship between manager and employee on television, in newspaper articles, and in the workplace is often negative. At TAG, we see the same thing in our work with organizations when we ask our audience to raise their hands if they ever had a bad manager—most people raise their hands. When we ask if they ever had a good manager, far fewer hands are raised.

What people are exposed to in the workplace on a consistent and ongoing basis has an impact on what they take as reality. Having a deep and meaningful connection with a manager is not the historical experience of most employees. It is *not* the reality, nor even remotely on the agenda. By stating this fact, I am not suggesting that there are pervasive, hostile, or unfriendly environments in most workplaces—not at all. What I am saying is that even when status has been suspended, and managers and employees are seeking to serve each other, there still remains a historical experience, a negative reality to overcome, that impedes how managers and employees connect.

Ethan Burris, Assistant Professor of Management at the McCombs School of Business at the University of Texas at Austin, writes about this disconnect[2]: "A lot of managers think that if they treat their staff respectfully and tell them 'my door is always open,' that should be enough to make their employees trust them." Not so, Burris says. "Our research shows that employees need more than that in order to feel safe to speak up." He continues, "Almost everyone I've talked to has felt some level of discomfort in speaking the truth to power."

This research and TAG's own experience confirm that a prevailing distrust exists between manager and employee. Both parties have work to do in order to establish a new reality in which intentional conversations can occur. Burris, in examining conversation patterns in credit unions, illustrates how evident this disconnection between manager and employee is in the workplace. In his research, Burris maps out each employee-to-employee conversation. His maps show when and how often an employee spoke up with a new idea to another employee. The research finds that employees are more likely to share a new idea with another employee than with a manager. In one study, his maps show that employees are *twelve times more likely* to share a new idea with a coworker than with a manager. Burris notes, "If managers are central in the communication networks of their work unit, they stand a good chance of hearing about problems and opportunities for improvement. But if they aren't central, it may indicate that they are out of the loop. At best, they are dependent on other employees to hear about what's going on in their department. At worst,

> BOTH PARTIES HAVE WORK TO DO IN ORDER TO ESTABLISH A NEW REALITY IN WHICH INTENTIONAL CONVERSATIONS CAN OCCUR.

it means important information is not reaching the key decision-makers of the organization."

This failure in the flow of communication that many organizations suffer from is historical and due, in part, to a flaw in the original model of "the manager." The manager's role, when the idea of working in an industrial organization was still new, was constructed around the idea that people needed to be managed if the work was going to get done. This construct often presumed that people really did not like to work, but would work if paid to do so and made to follow a set of norms. Hence, the role of the manager was to enforce the rules through regular conversation, to ensure that the company was getting "a full day's work for a full day's pay." So, over time, the conversation that the manager became known for having with employees was specific to the tasks and activities necessary to get work done.

We have certainly updated the way managers and employees are expected to interact in the twenty-first century. We have hundreds of books that address and dispel the old models of management that no longer work. We have laws, policies, and commissions to rid our organizations of abusive and unfair treatment. We have removed many of the barriers and put many strategies and processes in place to ensure safe and healthy workplaces. And yet one important vestige of the old still remains: this perceived barrier, this disconnect, between manager and employee that inhibits free-flowing, spontaneous, and collaborative conversations.

So what can be done to break the pattern of disconnection between manager and employee? Managers and employees must *rethink* everyday conversation. In many organizations, conversation flows at a shallow depth as managers and employees interact on the basis of an "us versus them" frame of mind. In contrast, in workplaces where deeper exchanges occur regularly, TAG has noticed a distinct difference in how managers and employees relate to each other. In these instances, managers and employees have free-flowing, spontaneous, and constructive conversations—they have intentional conversations.

The manager-to-employee relationship in these situations is a reciprocal one—both parties support each other. Managers and employees function seamlessly as a productive unit. These organizations have engaged workplaces because their managers and employees know how to cultivate connection. People who cultivate connection demonstrate that they care for the other person during the conversation. If you were to go back to the earlier chapter and look at the people in this book who were highlighted as modeling intentional conversations, you will see that the connection deepened during their conversations, as both parties were giving and receiving. In a way, it's like the cycle of nature—as we cultivate the soil, the soil in turn nourishes the seed and returns our food back to us. To cultivate connection, the same kind of cycle is at play—you give to the other person, and he or she in turn gives to you.

Too many of our conversations flow at the shallow depth of "What's in it for me?" In an intentional conversation we elevate our thinking to "What can I give to this person during this exchange?" As you enter into a conversation with someone, think in terms of making a deposit or accepting a gift. That's what the best managers and employees do—they cultivate connection by giving and receiving. Heather and her food services employee, and Jim and the troublesome Ms. Brash, demonstrated this third step in the SECRET—they offered gifts to the other and accepted the gifts that were offered to them in return. They cultivated connections. Heather, without knowing it, gave her employee a reason to go on living, and when the employee received her gift, she reciprocated with her gratitude and outstanding effort at work. Jim gave Ms. Brash the opportunity to discover what it was she did well; Ms. Brash in turn gave Jim the benefits of her expertise and the joy of mentoring her as she became a positive role model of individual growth and development.

This action step, *cultivate connection*, may seem a bit soft, even "touchy-feely," to some who may have been taught that management and work should be practical and unfeeling. You may have even been taught that, as a manager, you need to keep distance between you and the employee. And, as an employee, you have probably been taught to stay in your place and to defer and submit to the authority of the manager. The underlying reason for what you have learned still applies: there are distinct roles that manager and employee must play in order for an organization to succeed. However, organizations perform at their highest levels when those roles work together as a united whole, manager and employee in sync, taking and surrendering authority in tandem.

A few years ago, the United States Army was challenged to experience this kind of synchronicity during a retreat facilitated by Joe Jurkowski and Kevin Ford of TAG Consulting. Joe shares his experience that day here:

> The Army Chief of Staff had commissioned a study entitled "The Army Transformation" and we were there to help the generals work through the results of the study . . . We had carefully studied the data in the report to prepare to facilitate the discussion with the generals, but won-

dered about the results. From our view, the data reflected reorganization and not transformation.

From the moment we opened the session, chaos broke out in the room. These men were extremely disappointed with the study and they let us know about it in no uncertain terms. Most of them felt the report was useless and did not address the most serious underlying problems the Army was facing. My partner and I realized we had lost the room almost before we even started. These men were angry, and neither my partner nor I knew what to do. In desperation, I asked a question: "Who among you will tell the Army Chief of Staff what you think about the study?" Immediately there was silence. These are some of the bravest, most dedicated men you will ever meet. They had been in combat and faced death, and yet when asked to tell their superior what they thought and what he needed to hear, no one volunteered. Finally, after several minutes of silence, one three-star general raised his hand and asked me if I would tell the Chief of Staff that the study he had commissioned and paid an enormous sum of money for was useless.

At that moment, everyone realized that Army Transformation first meant having the conversations that are critical to the well-being of the Army and the United States. For these men who had spent their lives in a command-and-control environment, facing their superior

> THE GOOD NEWS IS THAT EVERYONE CAN LEARN HOW TO HAVE AN INTENTIONAL CONVERSATION.

was more difficult than facing battle.

For a team that is not used to having them, intentional conversations can actually be so frightening that they immobilize the bravest of hearts, as you can see from Joe's report above. For many people in the workplace, even those with authority, the danger of attempting to have a robust, collaborative, and transparent conversation around a failure or misstep is formidable. The good news is, with guidance and a willing attitude, everybody can learn how to have an intentional conversation. Kevin Ford tells the rest of the Army retreat story as follows:

> It was late into the final day, two days after Joe had his experience, that he and I decided it was time to challenge the Corp leadership to have an intentional conversation about its failure to implement its own five-hundred-page strategic plan. It was an unexpected but pivotal breakthrough.
>
> "Everyone in this room," we said, "is aware of a hidden dynamic that has been tearing down the morale and productivity of this organization. Yet no one was willing to confront it yesterday. Are you willing to confront it today?"
>
> It was amazing the difference a day made . . . there was a spontaneous reaction to our question. One by one, going all the way around the circle, every person in the group responded, taking full responsibility for his or her own contribution to the failed implementation of the strategic plan.
>
> "In my own mind," said one, "I was blaming the CO

for not implementing the plan. Fact is, I am the bottleneck. I wasn't carrying out my responsibilities. It was easier to lay the blame on my manager than to do what needed to be done."

"I should have shown more leadership and initiative," admitted another. "Instead, I deferred to the commander. I see now that leadership isn't supposed to be invested in one person. In one way or another, we're all expected to show leadership. From now on I will."

The conversation ran deep; finally the commander spoke up and granted responsibility for driving the strategic plan forward to one of his subordinates. Within a month, with fresh leadership, the plan was being implemented.

This is why SECRET works: each step safely moves the conversation to a deeper and deeper level. In step one, *suspend status*, one person opens the door for intentional conversation by using words and actions that show they are on equal footing with the other person—no rank, class, or status difference. In step two, *empower each person*, a change in attitude opens the door for people to serve each other. In step three, *cultivate connection*, each person accepts the other's overture and invitation in order to connect on a deeper level. They both must be willing and able to give and to receive. But why? What is the reason for engaging at this deeper level? Judith Glaser, the author

> AN INTENTIONAL CONVERSATION TAPS INTO RESOURCES THAT ARE ALREADY THERE AND REVEALS THEM SO THAT THEY MAY BE PUT TO USE.

and researcher we mentioned earlier, provides this reply:

> When colleagues work in concert, they learn from each
> other, develop higher-level skills and wisdom, meet per-
> formance goals, and turn breakdowns into breakthroughs.

An intentional conversation taps into resources that are already there and reveals them so that they may be put to use. It is like what a farmer does by tilling the soil—he frees up the nutrients by digging down below the encrusted earth to get to the fresh soil. The SECRET process helps us to break up the fallow ground, helps us remove the scar tissue of old and failing conversation behavior. It exposes and demonstrates our tenderness—the touchy-feely part of a healthy conversation that many people resist. Yielding and giving to another person is like that: it reveals our vulnerability. And it is vulnerability that is both the requirement and reward of an intentional conversation—for as we open our hands and hearts up to give, we are also opening them up to receive. This action step ushers a manager, employee, supervisor, subordinate, spouse, teacher, student—whomever—to a higher and deeper level of conversation. Each person begins to realize and own that he or she can have meaningful and mutually beneficial conversations and relationships by taking the risk to give and receive during an intentional conversation.

SECRET OPPORTUNITY #4

How is *cultivate connection* different from *suspend status*? Is cultivating a connection about giving, getting, or both? How do you cultivate a connection in your conversations?

Instead of accepting her offer to resign, Jim offered Ms. Brash the opportunity to help him with a project. Ms. Brash was surprised and a bit suspicious, Jim noted, but she relented and accepted his offer. What Jim did over the next six months illustrates perfectly how the SECRET of intentional conversation can help you rethink everyday conversations and transform your career and those of others.

No longer was she an intolerable employee to him, but more and more he began seeing her as an equal partner, as she began working harder to get along with others. Such is the power of suspending status—it not only levels the ground between us, but also expands the opportunity for us to learn more about each other.

HOW DID THESE ARMY GENERALS FAIL TO CULTIVATE
CONNECTIONS? HOW MIGHT THEY IMPROVE THEIR CON-
NECTIONS IN THE FUTURE?

ENDNOTES:

1. Gerbner, G, L Gross, M Morgan, and N Signorielli. "The 'Mainstreaming' of America: Violence Profile No. 11." *Journal of Communication.* 30, no. 3 (September 1980): 10-29. www.onlinelibrary.wiley.com/doi/10.1111/jcom.1980.30. issue-3/issuetoc.

2. The University of Texas at Austin. "Missing Voices: Companies that quiet employee opinions alienate workers and miss out on big ideas." September 7, 2009. www.utexas.edu/features/2009/09/07/employees/.

CHAPTER SIX

THE *R* IN SECRET

REFRAME REACTION: to manage our responses during the conversation in a way that ensures that the conversation moves forward.

Conversation has a purpose. There is a reason why each conversation begins. There is also a reason why a conversation stalls, spirals downward, or progresses on to the level of an intentional conversation. Conversations are dynamic. They start with one subject and then flow toward many others, eventually landing on the final takeaway from the conversation. Conversations progress or fail due to one reason—our reaction. During a conversation, we react spontaneously to what is being said. There is no way for us to know for sure beforehand what the other person will say next, so our reaction is almost always immediate and unplanned. Something that we say or that the other person says influences our reaction and, subsequently, the progress of the exchange. What happens during a conversation and the message we take away from a conversation is due to our reaction.

The fourth word and the very important next step in the SECRET process is *reframe*—reframe reaction. To have an *intentional conversation*, everyone (and, in the context of this book, managers and employees) needs to know how to reframe reaction. In the *reframe reaction* step, we manage our reaction during the conversation in a way that ensures that the conversation progresses forward. Sometimes this is easy to do, and other times it is more difficult, as in the case below:

A few years ago, Larry, a consultant friend of mine, was speaking to a group of chief executive officers, members of a well-known industry organization in Orlando, Florida. About fifteen minutes into his speech, as he was walking among the audience of one thousand CEOs, Larry stated: "You are likely to be facing the same degree of difficulty in recruiting and hiring the smartest and brightest candidates as other industries."

Just as Larry made that statement, Mark, a CEO from Montana, stood up and responded that he did not believe the statement to be true. He then added, "And why don't you go back where you came from?" My friend Larry told me he was initially stunned and taken aback, but then thought that he must have misunderstood the last part of Mark's statement, so he asked him what he meant by that. Mark, moving closer to my friend—who is originally from another country and of a different race than Mark and most of the others in the room—said once again, "I do not agree with you. I think you need to go back where you came from."

At this point, before we go on, let me remind you that conversation is the spoken exchange of ideas, thoughts, and information between two or more people. So, Mark and Larry were indeed having a conversation. Let me also remind you, however, that *intentional conversation* requires that the conversation be carried out *with collaborative and mutually productive intent.* When a person initiates a conversation with us, as Mark stood up to do with Larry, we get to decide what happens next. We can react in one of three ways: have the conversation, ask for time to prepare to have that conversation, or refuse to have the conversation at all. In any case, our reaction is typically based upon the following intuitive criteria:

- **The value of the exchange to us.** We tend to have conversations with people with whom we *want* to have an exchange. Someone once said we do not have enough time to do everything we *need* to do, but we have all the time we need to do what we *want* to do. Likewise, we do not have enough time to have a conversation with everyone we meet, but we make enough time to speak with those with whom we wish to exchange an idea, thought, or piece of information.
- **The importance of the subject to us.** Once we decide to enter into the exchange, we begin assessing the importance of the subject to us.
- **The time we are willing to give to the exchange.** Based upon how important the subject is to us, we determine how much time we are willing to spend in the conversation.
- **The depth of relationship we have or wish to have with the person.** We assess what bearing the subject has upon the relationship that already exists between us or upon the one that we are hoping to develop.
- **The lasting potential impact of the exchange.** Finally,

during the conversation, we are constantly assessing the potential longevity of the conversation. Does this conversation have importance only for this moment, or does it matter in some way to my future, or to those of others?

Having an intentional conversation requires being mindful of both your needs and those of the other person. Intentional conversations happen within the context of a mutually beneficial exchange. Each person is intent on helping the other succeed, which is why the *reframe reaction* step is fourth in the progressive process of the SECRET formula. The *reframe reaction* step is where your conversation Return on Investment (ROI) truly begins. This is the stage when we begin to recognize and reap the benefits of the investment we have made in the conversation thus far. In steps one, two, and three, manager and employee have invested time, effort, and risk. Once both parties have participated in suspending status, empowering each person, and cultivating connection, a mutual investment has been made. By step four we have "skin in the game." We have given enough in exchange during the previous three steps to be interested in a good return. At this point, we care how the conversation ends.

HAVING AN INTENTIONAL CONVERSATION REQUIRES BEING MINDFUL OF BOTH YOUR NEEDS AND THOSE OF THE OTHER PERSON.

That is why we insist that this sequence is so important in the SECRET process. We need the previous steps to be accomplished in order to move on to the next step. First, we let people know that we value them as equal and not beneath us (*suspend status*). Then, we serve others instead of looking to be served (*empower each person*). Once we have established level ground and created an atmosphere of mutual service to each other, we then give and receive permission to build a valuable relationship (*cultivate connection*). We only get that permission when we have moved from a superficial "us versus them" level to a more in-depth reciprocal relationship. Once we start to go deeper, we become more reciprocal, which increases our desire for a mutually beneficial outcome from our conversation. To achieve the desired outcome, both parties now must be willing to monitor and modify their responses during the conversation to ensure there is continuous forward movement. That is the *reframe reaction* step.

Let me illustrate how this looks as we go back to the story of my friend Larry and his challenger. Larry, a black man from the Caribbean, had been challenged by Mark a second time when he said, "Why don't you go back where you came from?"

Larry, laying on a thicker island accent than he usually has, replied to Mark, "Why do you say that, mon?"

This light-hearted and jovial response caught Mark off guard. But when a small smile broke on Mark's face, the rest of the audience, glad for the comic relief, laughed loudly and freely. Larry had successfully engaged the SECRET process by getting Mark to momentarily suspend (perceived) status. Then, Larry proceeded to empower Mark; he respected his opinion, which led to the next step, *cultivate connection*. He solicited Mark's input; he asked Mark if he wanted to poll his peers to see if they agreed or disagreed with the statement that Larry had made about the degree of difficulty in recruiting and hiring the smartest and brightest candidates. Mark actually agreed that would be a good idea. The handheld electronic polling system that each participant had showed that 80 percent of the CEOs agreed with Larry's recruitment and retention statement. Now it was up to Mark whether he would engage in an intentional conversation or not. To do so, he would have to take the next step in the SECRET process—he would have to reframe his reaction. He did; he asked for the microphone and apologized before his peers to Larry for his inappropriate remarks. The atmosphere was clearer and even more collegial than before.

Sometimes we say things we do not mean. Sometimes we say things we do not mean to *say*. Whether it is what we have said, or what has been said to us, knowing how to reframe reaction gives us the opportunity to have an intentional conversation. Mastering this step will equip you to become the resident SECRET technician in your organization.

There are often situations like the one with Larry and Mark where an intentional conversation may seem unlikely, even impossible at first. But these are sometimes the ones where the greatest and most remarkable career, culture, and relationship changes can happen. Based upon our experience with clients across industries and around the world, my colleagues and I promise you this can be the case for you and your team. We can assure you of this because TAG's experience and practice with thousands of cases have proven that even when an intentional conversation between manager and employee seemed impossible, if you follow the concepts of SECRET applied in sequence, the process works. It works even in the worst workplace environments as illustrated below.

"He was choking her," she said. "He had his hand around her neck and he was choking her." Lucy, our client, was recounting to my fellow TAG consultants and me a recent incident in which a surgeon had actually left swollen, red fingerprint marks on the neck of a nurse. Lucy, the medical director of a prominent medical institution, was relating this story to us as a way of showing us how hostile the environment was in this workplace. Lives were literally at risk there, both those of the staff as well as those of the patients. Dysfunction was rampant. Lawsuits were mounting. Morale was extremely low.

Conversation was abrasive at best, and at its worst hostile. This was not a workplace where anybody dared or wanted to have an intentional conversation. And it was exactly because of those desperate conditions in this hospital years ago that we learned so much about teaching managers and employees how to use conversation to build a collaborative and productive workplace. Through this assignment, and through others before and after, we've developed and unpacked the SECRET process, which works even when people are so angry or intimidated that they are unable to have even the briefest of conversations without a fight.

As we worked to help this team of professionals, we were reminded again of the difference between being intentional in a conversation and having an *intentional conversation*. A person can be intentional in a conversation by being vindictive, evil, untruthful, or by committing a variety of other malicious acts. People in this hospital were being intentional; too many were intent upon doing harm to each other. In contrast, having an intentional conversation is, as I define it, the spoken exchange of ideas, thoughts, and information between two or more people *with collaborative and productive intent.*

At this medical institution, fear cascaded down the levels of employees. Doctors feared their own supervisors and referred to them as "the administration." They told us that the administration was just waiting for an opportunity to fire each and every one of them. They were convinced that there was a move afoot to dismiss the entire medical staff and bring in a whole new cadre of recently graduated doctors. The nurses also feared for their careers, but their fear was based more upon the concern that the doctors they worked with would commit some lethal mistake, taking a patient's life, and that somehow they would get the blame. The technicians were fearful of retaliation because more than one of them had filed harassment charges against the doctors. The managers were indignant, adamant, and not in the least bit interested in giving up authority to a group of, in their words, "lazy, incompetent, complaining employees."

To begin the work, we met again with Lucy and told her our plan. We told her we intended to have a series of conversations with each doctor, nurse, head of department, and technician. She worried that such a plan was going to do nothing but stir up even more complaints and frustration.

We let her know that this approach had been successful in other very challenging situations. At the time, we did not feel it was necessary to tell her that hers was the single worst workplace situation that we had ever encountered. While there have been volatile situations since our work with that hospital, up until then it was for us, at TAG, by far the most hostile, violent, and dangerous environment we had ever experienced. Reluctantly, she gave us permission to execute our plan with the caveat that she would cancel the contract if employee conditions got worse than they were already. We had a different worry—the only real risk was that things were already so bad that real change might not be possible. So it was not surprising that our first moves were met with skepticism—the environment was so chronically ill that anything that promised relief or healing was immediately suspect.

In this low-trust situation, we were hard-pressed to suggest the first step in the SECRET process. People are not likely to suspend status when they do not trust the other person. The employees, in similar fashion, were not interested in the third step; they had no appetite whatsoever to cultivate connection. They were angry and litigious. They wanted blood and suffering from those in charge. People needed to feel safer than they were feeling, and that was not happening because of the pervasive "loaded gun" management image held by employees and reinforced by the behavior of the supervisors.

Rumors began to circle that we were really hired by the administration to identify who was to be fired and who would be allowed to stay. We knew we had to change the conversation immediately. One thing we learned from this engagement is that immediate and transformational change can happen by getting people in crisis to the *reframe reaction* step as quickly as possible. This is the step during which people realize that conversation is transactional—that their action and reaction directly influences the outcomes of conversation. Managers and employees, in an intentional conversation, must take ownership of their reactions during conversation and, by doing so they can change the conversation outcome.

Nancy was the nurse manager in charge of a unit where employees were both victims and perpetuators of the dysfunction at this hospital. Several of the employees in this unit were on individual development plans due to misbehavior. Others within the unit were awaiting decisions on harassment charges they had filed against their supervisors. Yet, what we did with Nancy and her employees became the model for all the other units. We assigned *reframe your reaction* as homework for every person in the unit. Rather than try to apply this concept first in a specific conversation with their employee (or their manager), their assignment was to describe what their reaction had been when they had conversations in the past with their employee or manager. This was all done one-on-one with our consultants and kept confidential. We then asked them to generate a list of what ideal, productive, and collaborative reactions would look like compared to their actual reactions. While each group worked on these assignments in private, we simultaneously began laying the foundation for the eventual application of the fourth step by teaching them steps one, two, and three of the SECRET process.

With managers, we conducted sessions where they were taught how to change their approach from an "I'm the boss of you" status to behavior that demonstrated that they wanted to become a partner in helping the employee succeed. We also conducted sessions with employees, teaching them how to establish an initial connection with their manager by doing something as simple as inviting the manager to sit with them at lunch. At the same time, we had brainstorming sessions around what service to each other could look like.

Within two months, the managers in Nancy's unit had learned how to suspend status and had, in fact, begun to level the ground between themselves and the employees. They were now starting to do things to empower each other and their employees. Employees and managers, with our facilitation, now allowed for and cultivated a deeper, more reciprocal relationship. To their credit, each group invested the time, energy, and risk to take the next steps. Together, the people in this organization had now built enough of a foundation for us to start the transforming work of *reframe reaction*. Eighteen months had passed, and this hospital was a safer place for all.

When taking the *reframe reaction* step, you understand and

esteem the value of a positive, free-flowing, continuous exchange. You establish that you want the conversation to continue to progress and deepen. You demonstrate vested interest in building a relationship that is more than superficial—one that is durable enough to endure the unexpected twists and turns of everyday conversation.

SECRET OPPORTUNITY #5

How is *reframe reaction* different from *cultivate connection*?

Remember: When a person initiates a conversation with us, we get to decide what happens next by basing our reaction upon the following intuitive criteria:

- The value of the exchange to us.
- The importance of the subject to us.
- The time we are willing to give to the exchange.
- The depth of relationship we have or wish to have with the person.
- The lasting potential impact of the exchange.

IS *REFRAME REACTION* POSSIBLE WITHOUT THE FIRST
THREE STEPS? HOW? IF NOT, WHY NOT?

CHAPTER SEVEN

THE SECOND *E* IN SECRET

ENFORCE ENGAGEMENT: to insist that your ideas, thoughts, and information are received and acted upon.

Conversation is a learned behavior. We are not born talking—it's a "learn as you go" sort of thing. We pick up the rules over time as we hear and observe other people having conversations. According to language researchers Charles Temple, Ruth Nathan, Frances Temple, and Nancy Burris, children as young as two and three years old, as they learn to talk, begin figuring out the rules of conversation as they observe others and formulate rules for themselves. In their book *The Beginnings of Writing*, they make this observation:

Children seek from their early days to make sense of the communication around them. As their minds mature, they attempt—through a sort of gradual trial-and-error process—to construct a system of rules that will allow them to produce sentences like those they hear others use. Clearly, when children construct language rules, they are attempting to find rules or patterns that account for the language used by others in their presence. It is as if they were carefully feeling and probing the language to find its joints and seams, its outer shape and its inner workings.[1]

It is by trial and error, mimicking others, figuring out the rules, and putting words and sentences together for ourselves that we end up "learning" how to have everyday conversation. By the time we are seven years old, we know the rules by which to have conversation. Sadly, most people—including managers and employees—live their entire lives without learning to apply the rules of an intentional conversation. Up to this point, we have only referred to the SECRET process as action steps, but they are also rules that must be followed if one is to have an intentional conversation.

The fifth word and next step that must be practiced in the SECRET process is *enforce*—Enforce engagement. Sound a bit strong? Absolutely! At this stage in the conversation, you have paid your dues, you have done the hard work of suspending status, empowering others, cultivating connection, and reframing reaction. You are at the place in the conversation where it is now appropriate that you assert (and insist) that your ideas, thoughts, and information are valued and acted upon. This is a difficult and uncomfortable action step for many. But be encouraged; this step, once applied, can bring immediate and memorable results.

This was the case for the passengers, including myself, on United Flight 3774 from Minneapolis to Washington D.C. Entering the plane a bit ahead of me, a passenger spoke to the flight attendant who was standing at the door. The passenger was concerned about the two inches of snow that had collected on the plane.

Marieka, the flight attendant, responded by saying to the passenger, "He is standing right behind you."

The passenger, not understanding her meaning, said, "That's okay, he can wait. I just want to know that this plane will be de-iced prior to takeoff."

The man quietly standing just behind the passenger was actually

THROUGH INTENTIONAL CONVERSATION, WE INSIST THAT CRITICAL AND IMPORTANT ISSUES GET THE FOCUSED ATTENTION AND ACTION THAT WE DESIRE.

Captain Jason Gray, who had just come back from his pre-flight check. Having overheard the conversation, he spoke up and assured the passenger, "No problem, sir, I got it covered." The man nodded and proceeded to his seat.

About fifteen minutes after we had been seated, Captain Gray made this announcement: "Folks we are almost ready to depart. Before we depart, we will be de-icing the plane. This is the process: first you will see that they spray an orange-colored solution on the plane—this is to take the existing ice off the plane. Then they will apply the solution a second time—this is to keep the ice off the plane. You should actually smell the solution once the process gets started. Thank you for your concern, and we appreciate your trust. Your safety is our number one concern."

I was especially grateful for this experience for two reasons. First, I was grateful that Marieka and Captain Gray had accepted the challenge of having an intentional conversation. Second, I was especially grateful for the passenger who enforced engagement from others. Let me explain.

No doubt, the de-icing was already scheduled and was going to happen regardless of the passenger asking about it. But just the same, everybody on that plane benefited from the additional information and assurance that resulted from this intentional conversation. Through intentional conversation, we insist that critical and important issues get the focused attention and action that we desire. Captain Gray, Marieka, and the concerned passenger, through their brief but intentional exchange, identified, discussed, and acted upon an important, potentially life-threatening issue. In this example—and any time where there is an intentional conversation—the parties concerned, as well as others, benefit from enforced engagement.

Passengers on another flight were not so fortunate. The conversation that ensued prior to their flight did not have the crucial *enforce engagement* step of an intentional conversation.

January 13, 1982—a Boeing 737 prepared to take off from National Airport in Washington, D.C. Air Florida Flight 90 to Fort Lauderdale was running two hours late because of the icy conditions. As the plane idled, the co-pilot and the pilot were engaged in a conversation. This is the actual transcript of the fateful conversation:[2]

> **Co-pilot:** "Look how the ice is just hanging on the tail of that plane—see that?"
> **Pilot:** "Yeah."

Co-pilot: "It's been a long wait since the last de-icing."

Pilot: (silence)

Co-Pilot: "A lot of time for new ice buildup in this storm. You know this is a losing battle, trying to de-ice these things. It just gives you a false sense of security."

Pilot: (no response)

Moments later the plane was cleared for takeoff. The plane sped down the runway and started to climb.

Co-pilot: "Look at that indicator! That doesn't seem right, does it?"

Pilot: (silence)

Co-pilot: "Uh, that's not right."

Pilot: "Yes it is . . . there's eighty."

Co-pilot: "No, I don't think that's right . . . well, maybe it is . . . I don't know."

The stall warning began to sound. The plane stopped climbing and began falling back toward the ground.

Pilot: "Come on! Forward! Climb! Climb!"

Ten seconds of silence.

Co-pilot: "Larry, we're going down! Larry—!"

Pilot: "I know it—!"

Those were the last words on the cockpit voice recorder. Four people were killed in their cars on the 14th Street Bridge as the plane crashed into the Potomac, killing the pilot, co-pilot, and seventy-six others. The co-pilot had logged many hours flying in wintry conditions. The pilot had zero hours flying in such conditions. The pilot and the other souls on that plane needed the co-pilot to *enforce engagement*—to assert and insist that his ideas, thoughts, and information were received and acted upon. That is the power of this fifth step: being heard and getting a validating response.

In this instance, the co-pilot, with his many flight-hours flying in snowy weather, had the information needed to prevent this tragedy. He failed at the fifth step of the SECRET process. He failed to enforce engagement—to ensure that the other party is receiving and responding to the pertinent message.

> MOST CONVERSATIONS LACK THE BOLDNESS OF AN INTENTIONAL CONVERSATION, AND AS A RESULT LACK THE CLARITY THAT IS NEEDED TO CHANGE BEHAVIOR.

In an everyday conversation, we are usually satisfied with the clues that indicate our message is being received attentively. In an intentional conversation, we not only need to know that the other person is paying attention, but we are also looking for *confirmation* that our message has been received and that the required action will be taken. This was the position that the passenger on my flight from Minnesota took as he boarded the plane—"I need to be assured that this plane will be de-iced prior to takeoff." By insisting on this, he enforced engagement from both the flight attendant and the captain. The co-pilot on Air Florida Flight 90 could have said exactly the same thing: "I need to be assured that this plane will be de-iced prior to takeoff." He did not—he and the pilot did not have an intentional conversation. The co-pilot was hinting at his concern, but never came out directly and required that specific action be taken. They were talking, even exchanging ideas and thoughts, but their conversation lacked the boldness and clarity that the *enforce engagement* step requires.

When we enforce engagement, we take bold steps to be heard, and we follow through to ensure that our message is clear and is acted upon. Most conversations lack this type of boldness, and as a result, lack the clarity that is needed to change behavior. The *enforce engagement* step changes our behavior in that we say what needs to be said at the moment it needs to be said in order to get the results we need. At this stage, we challenge assumptions that are unclear or seem unfounded. We introduce ideas or information that clarify and redirect the focus of discussion. The *enforce engagement* step is where both parties get in sync with each other.

Let me go through this step again. To enforce engagement, we build on the work that has been done already through the first four steps. We would have already suspended status in the conversation. We would have found ways to serve each other. We would have also established a deeper, more reciprocal relationship. And we would have demonstrated that we value a positive and mutually beneficial result by being mindful of our reaction. Because we have already invested in the first few steps in the process, we are prepared and permitted to enforce engagement from the other person.

We owe it to the other party to be engaged in the conversation. And we owe it to ourselves to require *them* to engage with us. Yet, we often allow disengagement from the other person or practice disengagement ourselves when we are in conversation. We check out, shut down, become distracted—and the other party knows it. This is not the case when we practice intentional conversation. People in an intentional conversation freely hold each other accountable. They insist upon being heard. They invite immediate and honest feedback. They care enough about the conversation outcome to demand attentiveness and candor. And people who practice intentional conversation accept accountability. They, in fact, expect to be held accountable, emotionally and psychologically, during the conversation. They embrace the *enforce engagement* step. They do this because they know it is crucial to the collaborative and productive intent of an intentional conversation. They know that both parties must *co-labor* in order for the conversation to yield the best possible results. No one is allowed to be a spectator or sit idly by in the *enforce engagement* step—everybody participates.

It is in achieving this degree of mental intimacy and shared commitment that makes this step the most pivotal of all the steps in the entire SECRET process. This is where the meeting of the minds occurs, where the synthesizing of ideas and the solidifying of shared purpose happens. This is where change occurs. Here, we change our minds or those of others. We change how people feel, and we see our own feelings change. We birth new ideas and surrender old and outdated ones. It is this step that you cannot afford to miss or shy away from in your significant conversations. For it is at this point in conversation, when we have the option to enforce engagement, when we make the kinds of decisions that haunt or delight us for the rest of our lives.

How about you, how do you participate in conversation? Are you a passive or an active participant? Do you dare to enforce engagement in your conversation? Many people will find this step challenging. It is challenging because a different set of rules, unrehearsed rules—rules that are rarely practiced—are required in order to have an intentional conversation. Remember, as children, we learn the rules of conversation. In the same way, through the rules of the SECRET process, we learn how to practice an *intentional conversation*. Once we follow the first four rules of *suspend status, empower each person, cultivate connection,* and *reframe reaction,* this fifth rule, *enforce engagement,* is relatively easy to obey. It is easy because, through the process, we have built the conversation up to where it is vitally important that we are being heard. Secondly, once we establish that we are indeed being heard, the nature of the conversation we have created ensures that we also want to hear and understand the other person. This step takes reciprocity to another level—the willing, yielding, and taking of authority by each person. This is reciprocity on steroids!

So, how do we do the *enforce engagement* step? We do it by giving permission to each other to *interrupt, redirect, question,* and *push back* during the conversation. By doing this, we set ourselves up to begin to identify and select the takeaways that result from the exchange. Here is the takeaway from this chapter: the *enforce engagement* step requires us to be assertive and mindful, for it is at that point when we make crucial and critical decisions that can affect us for the rest of our lives.

SECRET OPPORTUNITY #6

What is a recent conversation you had in which you enforced engagement? How?

When we enforce engagement, we take bold steps to be heard, and we follow through to ensure that our message is clear and is acted upon. At this stage, we challenge assumptions that are unclear or seem unfounded. We introduce ideas or information that clarify and redirect the focus of discussion. The *enforce engagement* step is where both parties get in sync with each other.

WITH WHOM ARE YOU LIKELY TO HAVE A CONVERSATION IN WHICH YOU NEED TO ENFORCE ENGAGEMENT? WHAT STEPS IN THE SECRET PROCESS HAVE YOU DONE OR NEED TO DO IN ORDER TO HAVE PERMISSION TO ENFORCE ENGAGEMENT?

ENDNOTES:

1. Temple, Charles, Ruth Nathan, Nancy Burris, and Frances Temple. *The Beginnings of Writing*. 3rd ed. Pearson, 1992.

2. Aircraft Recording. "CVR Transcript for the Crash of Air Florida Flight 90." AVweb. December 23, 1999. www.avweb.com/news/safety/182404-1.html.

CHAPTER EIGHT

THE *7* IN SECRET

> **TRIAGE TAKEAWAYS:** to prune and select what really matters from the clutter of ideas, thoughts, and pieces of information that make up the deluge of everyday conversations.

onversation is a selective process. It is like a refiner's fire, a potter's lathe, and a farmer's threshing floor. The ideas, thoughts, and information presented during a conversation are instantly examined, tagged, and sorted by both parties. Some of the ideas, for example, get tagged in the "do not retain" group—these are discarded almost immediately. Other ideas are put into a "more conversation required" group—these may be discussed more right then or at a later time. Still other ideas are put into the "this is important, urgent, upsetting, and problematic" group, and from the moment they are uttered they become the passionate or focused subject for the rest of the exchange.

Every idea, thought, and bit of information shared during a

conversation gets filed in some way based upon the next step the person has decided to take. In this way, conversation is the refining, forging, and interpreting of messages we give and receive from each other. In essence, during each conversation, we are creating something new out of what the other person presents and we offer that back to the other person, who in turn does the same. This process can be a positive and productive cycle. Too often, however, it is not. Conversations spiral down. They deteriorate to the point where we lose the opportunity to take away new ideas, thoughts, and information from each other. This does not have to be the case; we can learn how to optimize every conversation by sorting and identifying important takeaways. The last word in the SECRET process and the next action step is *triage*—Triage takeaways. Triage is a crucial and immediate action step during a medical emergency. It saves lives by sorting patients with the most severe, life-threatening injuries for treatment first. Triage is every bit as serious and useful when it comes to conversation. As we have shown throughout this book, having the right conversation at the right time can save lives.

So how does this step fit in with the preceding steps? Remember that an intentional conversation is progressive—each step lays the foundation for and leads to the next step. An intentional conversation starts with the *suspend status* step. At the outset of a conversation, a spouse, parent, manager—or whoever has formal, perceived, or relational status—levels the social ground between the parties by suspending status. In the workplace, for example, a manager who takes this action step willingly disarms his or herself of "the loaded gun" and entreats the employee to enter into candid and spontaneous dialogue with them. The second step, *empower each person*, transfers the responsibility for the conversation outcome to both parties. Each person now facilitates a new way of thinking, that of serving the other person.

The third step, *cultivate connection,* requires mutual effort from both the manager and the employee to build and sustain a reciprocal relationship. In step four, *reframe reaction,* we change our perspective in order for the conversation to continue to progress and deepen. We are committed to a mutually beneficial outcome. In the fifth step, *enforce engagement,* we operate from a place of some authority within the conversation. We insist on and will settle for nothing less than full engagement from ourselves and from the other person. All of these action steps serve as building blocks for moving the conversation forward. In *triage takeaways,* this last step, the difference an intentional conversation makes is fully realized.

Conversations happen all the time without any positive difference being made. Any parent of a "typical" teenager, manager of an unmotivated workgroup, pastor of a complacent congregation, or spouse of a stubborn person knows that conversations happen all the time to no avail. Conversations sometimes feel like nothing more than wasted moments.

Daniel Kahneman, Nobel Laureate in economics, identified in his award-winning research that we experience about twenty thousand moments in a day.[1] If one out of every ten moments were spent in conversation, that amounts to two thousand times per day that we exchange ideas, thoughts, and information in conversation. What will have been accomplished at the end of a day for all this time and energy spent in conversation? That depends upon whether the conversations were merely an exchange of words or if any were at the level of an intentional conversation.

Intentional conversation, as the name suggests, brings intent to bear. The SECRET process demands intentionality. We have to practice intentionality—that is to say, we have to have specific intent—in order to have an intentional conversation. This last step, *triage takeaways*, adds intent to the way we prune and select what really matters from the clutter of ideas, thoughts, and pieces of information that make up the deluge of everyday conversations. Becoming intentionally selective and precise about which conversations (and what ideas within a conversation) deserve more or less of your energy is critical to your success as an employee, manager, parent, priest, or person. It may only take one conversation to make or break a career, to enhance or wreck a life. In the foreword of *Fierce Conversations* by Susan Scott, Ken Blanchard, renowned author and business expert, writes:

> The notion that our lives succeed or fail one conversation at a time is at once commonsensical and revolutionary. It is commonsensical because all of us have had conversations that, for better or worse, profoundly altered our professional or personal lives. It is revolutionary because a course on conversations won't be found in an MBA curriculum. Yet who among us hasn't spent time and energy cleaning up the aftermath of a significant but failed conversation? While success is often measured by an accumulation of titles, acquisitions, and the financial bottom line, little or no attention is paid to the power of each conversation to move us toward or away from our stated business and life goals.[2]

Conversation, as Blanchard says in the above paragraph, has the power to move us toward or away from our goals. To move forward, however, we need to know which conversations we should forgo and which ones we should not go without. This is the kind of realization that astronaut James A. Lovell wrote about on his Facebook page on February 21, 2015, as he shared this reflection:

> With the wisdom of hindsight, I should have said, "Hold it. Wait a second. I'm riding on this spacecraft. Just go out and replace that tank." But the truth is, I went along, and I must share the responsibility with many, many others for the $375 million failure of *Apollo 13*.
>
> On just about every spaceflight we have had some sort of failure, but in this case, it was an accumulation of human errors and technical anomalies that doomed *Apollo 13*.[3]

How many times have you felt you should have spoken up or should have had that one conversation? Lovell certainly felt that way. No doubt many others connected to the *Apollo 13* flight also felt that way. Many times when looking back, we see important and critical ideas that were spoken, warning thoughts we had, or anomalies that we overlooked. Why do we see clearer *after* the conversation? Why do we not act then and there during the conversation? Because that is not the way we have learned to have conversation. Remember, as children, we learn conversation by mimicking what we see others do. And what has been modeled for us thus far has taught us to wait our turn, speak within the confines of our status, do not risk offending, and go along to get along. It is this mindset we enter into conversations with that hinders what we observe and take away. We do not enter conversations mentally prepared to triage, to seek out and act upon the important and urgent ideas among the clutter. We do not—maybe we dare not—think triage. The triage way of thinking incites us to interrupt, stop, direct, and question based upon what is being shared in the exchange. Triage is a disrupting influence, but it is critical to the refining and distilling of the important and crucial takeaways.

When we prune and select our takeaways in conversation, we are like a triage nurse, deciding and directing the action we take. Triage determines which conversations or ideas get moved up for immediate attention, which ones can wait, and which ones get quick treatment and are dismissed right away. With the heavy traffic of conversations we have in any given week, it may seem likely that at least some intentional conversations occur. They do not. First, intentional conversations never *just* occur; intentional conversations have to be made to occur—you have to *make* them happen. Second, they do not simply occur because conversations require the other five action steps of the SECRET process and the *triage takeaways* step in order to have the elements of an intentional conversation. People are not inclined to have intentional conversations naturally. It is a learned behavior; however, most people never learn this behavior because it is so rarely modeled. Learning the SECRET process will greatly enhance your ability to identify and select the conversation or idea within the avalanche of everyday conversations that can transform your career and relationships.

So what does this step, *triage takeaways*, look like? Jack, a brilliant executive and leader in a large accounting firm, has just finished a meeting with his boss and other executives. During the meeting, one of Jack's employees gave a briefing on a large project Jack's team was doing for a client. Jack was a bit disappointed in the way the meeting had gone, but overall he felt he had done a good job at recovering the fumbles that his employee had made during his presentation. On the way out, Jack's boss was talking with another person but stopped just long enough to ask Jack to stop by his office some time later to discuss the meeting. Jack agreed. However, Jack got busy with several projects and forgot to go up to see his boss that day.

"But early the next day," Jack told our consultant, "my boss called me and asked me to come to see him right away. I went up to his office, and what he told me was revealing and disappointing." Jack discovered that his boss had a very different perspective on the meeting the day before. "My boss said to me, 'Yesterday, it was clear about fifteen minutes into his presentation that your employee was not as prepared as he should have been. What concerns me, Jack, is why did you, for forty-five minutes, continue to rip him to shreds?' I did not realize that was how I was com-

> A TRIAGE WAY OF THINKING POSITIONS US TO LOOK FOR THE PROBLEM, OPPORTUNITY, OR REASON FOR THE CONVERSATION.

ing across," Jack said as he continued, "Then my boss said to me, 'Jack, didn't you feel me kicking you under the table?' I really did not feel him kicking me under the table. I missed it completely."

Yes, Jack missed it—of course he did—because he did not yet know the SECRET of intentional conversation. Jack did not know how to use the *triage takeaways* step during the brief exchange with his boss the day before. The *triage takeaways* step teaches us to interrogate each conversation for what is crucial and pertinent. Jack, like all of us do sometimes, overlooked an important piece of information: his boss stopped his conversation with another person in order to ask Jack to come and see him. Jack did not pinpoint the crucial reason why his boss made sure he had that short conversation with him. A triage way of thinking positions us to look for the problem, opportunity, or reason for the conversation. Next, triage thinking leads us to generate options for solving the problem. Finally, triage thinking ensures that action is taken based upon the option selected. In an intentional conversation, these steps are being done even as the conversation evolves.

Later, when Jack was learning the SECRET process, he presented this particular conversation as a case study during the training. Here is what Jack told his small group:

"I totally missed the urgency my boss was expressing by interrupting his conversation in order to ask me to come to see him. That incident helped me to realize how I had been setting myself up for failure for a long time by the way I conducted conversations. I saw conversations as an opportunity to be sure I got my ideas across. I never thought of takeaways because that was not the reason I entered into conversations. I had conversations to make sure things got done. I was oblivious of all that was happening during the conversation. Triage and the importance of identifying takeaways was a foreign concept for me. I was a bull in a china shop. I used my status as manager as a platform to say whatever I felt like saying to those who reported to me. In this case, I thought that, as the boss of my fumbling employee, I had the right and responsibility to show that I had the answers that he did not have. By doing this often, I failed not only in that instance, but I failed consistently to create an environment where my employees would ever be able to have an intentional conversation with me."

Jack did learn the *triage takeaways* step and the entire SECRET process, and he shared a very different example with us a few months later.

Jack was having lunch with two of his employees, Greg and Jennifer, when Greg mentioned an action that had been taken on a project without Jack's approval. Both of them knew how angry Jack would get when he was not informed prior to such action. "However," Jack said to us, "this was a triage moment for me. Yes, he had misspoken, and normally I would confront him right there on the spot. But there were other more important and crucial things to discuss. So, I chose to ignore his comment and focus instead on what was more important. And, what was more important was for me to affirm the good work he and his team were doing. Both employees," Jack said, "were dumbstruck. And," he added, "I must admit it felt good to be able to turn that into a positive and uplifting moment for them."

When managers and employees learn how to have a *triage mindset*, the result is pervasive change. Everyone reaps the results when managers and employees engage fully and critically in conversation. This triage step is the most challenging for some people. It requires a degree of assertiveness that many people are not used to in conversation. But, remember that each step stands on the footing of the prior step. All along, by taking each action step, we have been building the base that makes it safe for us to become progressively more assertive.

Starting with the *reframe reaction* step, our approach builds upon the transformative and supportive action of steps one, two, and three by taking more directive and assertive action in steps four, five, and six. At the *reframe reaction* step, we are invested in the conversation, and we begin to take action to ensure we get results. The *enforce engagement* step likewise may cause a bit of discomfort for people, because once again it is a step that requires assertiveness. The *triage takeaways* step is, however, the most assertive, even to the point of interrupting or redirecting the conversation. Together, these three steps, in particular, present a huge departure from conversation norms. Conversation norms reinforce the benign behavior that leads to clutter: an exchange of a lot of words, a lot of ideas, and a lot of information with few real results or meaningful changes in the workplace or our relationships.

Intentional conversations go beyond the superficial and cursory. Intentional conversation leads to transformation. And that transformational exchange requires the scrutiny, selectivity, and critical questioning of the *triage takeaways* step. So how does the *triage takeaways* step work? To perform the *triage takeaways* step, just ask a one-worded question—why? A triage nurse in an emergency situation asks "why"—why should this person be treated next? A manager using triage takeaways asks "why"—why is this person saying thank you to me with tears in her eyes? An employee with a triage mindset might ask "why is my manager discounting each idea I am presenting?" Similarly, a spouse doing triage thinking asks "why"—why is he/she bringing up this same idea again? As you ask "why," you will find that you may need to get clarification and perspective from the other person. That is why the triage takeaways step and the entire SECRET process requires the assertiveness we began discussing in this chapter and the humility that we will discuss fully in the next chapter.

SECRET OPPORTUNITY #7

During your most recent conversation with your manager, did you use triage takeaways? How?

Remember that a triage way of thinking does three things:

- positions us to look for the problem, opportunity, or reason for the conversation.
- leads us to generate options for solving the problem.
- ensures that action is taken based upon the option selected.

In an intentional conversation, these steps are being done even as the conversation evolves.

DESCRIBE AN INCIDENT WHEN YOU OBSERVED SOMEONE HAVE OR WHEN YOU HAD A TRIAGE MINDSET.

ENDNOTES:

1. Kahneman, Daniel. *Thinking, Fast and Slow*. Farrar, Straus and Giroux, 2011.

2. Blanchard, Ken. "Foreword." Foreword. *Fierce Conversations: Achieving Success at Work & in Life, One Conversation at a Time*. New York: Berkley Books, 2004. Print.

3. Lovell, James A. Facebook post. February 21, 2015.

CHAPTER NINE

THE SECRET OF THE SECRET

Suspend Status

Empower Each Person

Cultivate Connection

Reframe Reaction

Enforce Engagement

Triage Takeaways

Now that you know the SECRET process, what exactly is the difference you can expect in your career and relationships? That depends on if you are willing to do what *you alone* can do from this point forward. We know the process works. If you were to stop right now and put to practice all that I have taught you thus far, you would experience positive improvements in your life and work. However, if you want to transform your life and career, you need to know the *secret* of the SECRET. No, there is nothing else to memorize—no more acronyms, no more theory. Just owning the secret of the SECRET is what is needed now.

When conversations happen, they happen because human need is at work. The need to have a conversation resides in us—it is innate. Every human, regardless of personality type, has a natural appetite to engage in conversation at some time or another. Some people have a greater and ever-present need to talk, while others have an infrequent and brief, to-the-point need. Because the need is present at some level in all humans, everyone will initiate or participate in a conversation at some time. But, as you have read throughout this book, having just a conversation is not enough for transformational change to take place. To see fundamental and significant change, you need to actively invest time and energy.

Bob Slocum, a manager in Joseph Heller's novel *Something Happened*, reveals much about himself and the passive approach he takes to his role when he says:

> In my department, there are six people who are afraid of me and one small secretary who is afraid of all of us. I have one other person working for me who is not afraid of anyone, not even me, and I would fire him quickly, but I'm afraid of him.[1]

A scene like the one above may not be your reality at work, but you may be in a similar quandary; you, like this manager, may be a victim of passivity. Bob, by his passivity, has allowed or enabled an environment of fear to develop, and as a result, finds that he himself lives in fear at work. In much the same way, without meaning to, most people take a passive approach to conversation. Passivity in conversation happens when we fail to examine how it is we *do* conversation. How do you do conversation? Have you ever thought about that? Chances are you do conversation just like most people do—the way you have seen it done, the way you have learned to do it. But have you ever examined if you needed to, or consciously determined that you will, do conversation differently? If, like most people I have asked, your answer is no, then you will benefit greatly from applying the SECRET process to your everyday conversations. Conversation in the conventional way is too often a passive exchange of ideas, thoughts, and information. Passivity in conversation happens too often as we put our mouths into action without really putting our brains into gear.

DOING CONVERSATION THE INTENTIONAL DIFFERENCE REQUIRES A MIXTURE OF HUMILITY AND ASSERTIVENESS.

This passivity is due in great part to conversation being so natural to us that it requires little conscious effort. We do not see a need to work on our conversation—after all, we do it every day. To even think about working on conversation seems unnatural, maybe even ridiculous. However, to have a meaningful conversation—that is, an intentional conversation—you have to do conversation differently, and that takes focused action, not absentminded passivity.

Because it takes hard work, most people would rather avoid having conversation at a deeper level. It is so much easier to have superficial and trivial conversations than it is intentional ones. To have a strictly work-related conversation with a manager or employee does not demand much emotional energy. But to create an environment where people are safely dealing with real issues or spontaneously offering critical but positive feedback to others, that involves risk and vulnerability. For most people, that is a greater burden than they are willing to take on—and that is exactly why the SECRET process is so vital. The six action steps provide the ease and safety by which one can *do* conversation differently.

To do conversation the way we suggest in this book is to practice intentional conversation. To practice intentional conversation, use the six action steps in the following ways: use the first three steps, *suspend, empower,* and *cultivate,* to infuse humility into your conversation. Remember, when we do these three steps, we serve the other person. Use the last three steps, *reframe, enforce,* and *triage,* to apply your assertiveness. At this point in the conversation, we have earned the right to use enough firmness to ensure that both parties are getting what they need from the conversation. Doing conversation the intentional difference way requires a mixture of humility and assertiveness. It is this combination of humility and assertiveness that is not presently practiced in regular conversation. It is this fusing of two seemingly opposite traits that is foreign to and uncomfortable for most people. It is this crucible—this tension, the yielding and taking of authority—that many people struggle with in trying to have an intentional conversation. It requires balance.

Jim Collins, renowned author and business consultant, in his book *Good to Great,* alludes to this balancing as "a personal humility and fierce will and determination to achieve outcomes" possessed by those leaders whom he calls Level 5 leaders.[2] An article in *The Harvard Business Review* (July 2005 issue) articulated Collins's theory in this paragraph:

Collins argues that the key ingredient that allows a company to become great is having a Level 5 leader: an executive in whom genuine personal humility blends with intense professional will. To learn that such CEOs exist still comes as a pleasant shock. But while the idea may sound counterintuitive today, it was downright heretical when Collins first wrote about it—the corporate scandals in the United States hadn't broken out, and almost everyone believed that CEOs should be charismatic, larger-than-life figures. Collins was the first to blow that belief out of the water.[3]

Collins discovered that the combination of humility and assertiveness was the differentiator between the successful CEOs and the unsuccessful ones. In intentional conversation, this combination is likewise the difference maker. However, humility, especially in leaders or others in charge, has often been seen as weakness, timidity, and lack of confidence. Assertiveness is often experienced as bossy, domineering, and abrasive. Reducing the anxiety and doubt brought about by these two negative and prevalent views of humility and assertiveness and keeping them in perfect balance is the critical and core function of the SECRET process. People who will do conversation differently must trust and allow the process to create the environment and maintain the balance that is required for an intentional conversation to happen.

This was the challenge for Melena, the vice president of client services at one of the big three car manufacturers. Melena was the only woman out of fifty executives on the extended leadership team. Michael, her boss, was a hard-nosed, take-charge, egotistical person and he did not quite care that corporate had, in his words, sent him a "woman to babysit when there is so much serious work to do." Melena had a master's degree in engineering from Purdue University and was seen by many of the other executives as one of the most competent leaders in the organization. And she was, except when Michael was around—then she faltered.

"My brain just seems to shut down at the worst time," she said, "right when Michael asks me a question. In staff meetings, I do not remember a time when I was ever able to answer fast enough or smart enough for him. Once I hesitate, he quickly dismisses me and turns to someone else in the group for the answer, or he changes the subject." This was the case every time, right up until she understood how to balance humility and assertiveness through the SECRET process. Learning how to demonstrate both of these seemingly opposite traits at the same time, to good effect, is an important aspect of applying SECRET, but this is not the secret of the SECRET process.

So what *is* the secret of the SECRET? The SECRET does involve both humility and assertiveness, and when I continue the story about Melena and Michael, I will explain how these two apply. But before I reveal the secret of the SECRET, let us examine what SECRET is *not*. It is not about you. Having an intentional conversation is not solely about us, but about getting to know someone and letting ourselves become known to the other person. It is not about effective communication. The power of SECRET is not unleashed by choosing the right words, right tone, or right nonverbal behavior. These are important when trying to improve and repair communication—but that is not the approach of this book. The focus is upon the person and the choices they make concerning how they *do conversation*. Let's continue with what the SECRET is not:

- The SECRET is not about how to correct employee misbehavior.
- The SECRET is not about how to confront the underperformer.
- The SECRET is not about how to improve negotiation.
- The SECRET is not about how to have difficult conversations.

All of these are very good tactical discussions. They work well to repair broken communication by providing a script, a guide, or substitute words and phrases for a specific problem or situation. The potency of the SECRET is that it is *not* tactical. It is not remediation, but it is transformation—careers and lives are changed through this process. The SECRET process changes our *thinking* and *feeling* in order to change our *doing*. Melena learned the process, and it changed the way she interacted with Michael. Here is how she described her SECRET process with Michael to us at TAG:

> One day, a few months ago, I arranged to have a meeting with Michael. When I got to his office, he was standing looking out of his window with his back toward the door. I knocked, entered, and greeted him. Instead of turning around to face me, he continued looking out the window. I could feel the old nervous feelings reaching out for me. I started to fidget and squeezed the document I was holding. That's when I remembered the document I was holding was my plan for reducing the status differential. I had learned through the SECRET process that to help someone suspend status, the person wanting to help must empower themselves first. I believed the docu-

ment I held would help me help Michael. Michael finally turned around and acknowledged me with a nod. Then he told me that he had only a few minutes before his next meeting and so this will have to be a brief conversation. I told him I understood and that I appreciated him seeing me on short notice for a few minutes. I moved right into telling him why I wanted to talk to him, I said:

"Michael, I need your help please. I want to learn how to serve you and the team more effectively and I believe I have found just the tool that will help me to do that. Do you mind if I show you what I am talking about?" I said as I placed the document on the table.

His eyebrows arched ever so slightly, and I knew that I had gotten his interest. He replied, "As long as it is brief. Like I said, I have another meeting." I proceeded to show him how *The Engagement Guide©* (TEG) can be used to clarify and set expectations. What I did not say was how the TEG provided an easy and helpful way to begin a collaborative conversation between manager and employee. I took fifteen minutes of his time, and at the end, he suggested that we continue our conversation at another time. I agreed, but get this, as I was walking out the door, he said, "Be sure to talk to Jenny" (his assistant) "and get a date next week on my calendar. I want to hear more about how to use this tool. Thank you for coming to see me about this." I left there with an amazing feeling; I had never imagined that he and I could or would ever connect. Over the last three months, we have been meeting regularly, working through the TEG, and having other conversations about my unit and the business overall.

Humility, as Melena demonstrated, is *seeking permission to serve; assertiveness*, as she modeled, is *taking persistent, intentional action*. Melena successfully learned to do both, and it changed her career. When TAG last checked on her, she had been promoted to chief operations officer—by Michael.

In an intentional conversation, we seek and grant permission to suspend, empower, cultivate, reframe, enforce, and triage. Also, in an intentional conversation, we act with intentionality toward our status, each person, our connection, our reaction, our engagement, and the takeaways.

The SECRET, as you learned, is an acronym of six letters that represent six verbs that impact six objects: we suspend status, we empower each person, we cultivate connection, we reframe reaction, we enforce engagement, and we triage takeaways. It would be outstanding if you would memorize all of that and apply them to each and every one of your conversations—*not!* That will not be necessary or practical. All you need to remember is the acronym SECRET and the secret of SECRET. So, what is the secret?

The secret of the SECRET is this . . . *wait for it . . .*

CHANGE YOUR CONVERSATION BEHAVIOR!

The secret and the power of the SECRET lies entirely upon changing the way we *do* conversation. Conversation is a learned behavior—one that we have practiced for decades. It is second nature to us. We do it automatically, the way we have seen others do it. Now, however, you have the option to change how you do conversation. Starting now, enter into each and every conversation with the SECRET process in mind. Like Melena, Jim (the manager from the St. Paul Company), and others in this book, use the process to change the way you do conversation with your manager or employee. Use the SECRET to enhance your conversations with your spouse, your children, and your friends. At the beginning of any conversation, especially your significant conversations, just remember the SECRET and the secret of the SECRET: *change your conversation behavior.*

Also, remember that these two traits, humility and assertiveness, drive the activity and focus of the SECRET process. By exercising humility, each person asks for and grants permission in an intentional conversation. By applying assertiveness, each person momentarily assumes authority in an intentional conversation. Here is how humility and assertiveness relate to the six steps:

WE EXERCISE HUMILITY WHEN WE:	WE APPLY ASSERTIVENESS WHEN WE:
SUSPEND STATUS: We communicate in a way that values and esteems the other person as equal to or higher than ourselves.	**REFRAME REACTION:** We manage our responses during the conversation in a way that ensures that the conversation moves forward.
EMPOWER EACH PERSON: We serve the other person during conversation in a way that validates that we have their interests and well-being in mind.	**ENFORCE ENGAGEMENT:** We insist that our ideas, thoughts, and information are received and acted upon.

WE EXERCISE HUMILITY WHEN WE:	WE APPLY ASSERTIVE- NESS WHEN WE:
CULTIVATE CONNECTION: We create an environment of mutual giving and receiving in order to forge a deeper relationship.	**TRIAGE TAKEAWAYS:** We prune and select what really matters from the clutter of ideas, thoughts, and pieces of information that make up the deluge of everyday conversations.

Like any new behavior, exercising humility and applying assertiveness will take time and practice to achieve mastery. The good news is there are thousands of opportunities to practice every day. In the next chapter, we provide the opportunity for you to put your newfound knowledge to use and practice intentional conversations.

ENDNOTES:

1. Heller, Joseph. *Something Happened*. New York: Knopf, 1974.

2. Collins, James C. *Good to Great: Why Some Companies Make the Leap . . . and Others Don't*. New York: HarperBusiness, 2001.

3. Collins, Jim. "Level 5 Leadership: The Triumph of Humility and Fierce Resolve." *Harvard Business Review*. July 1, 2005. www.hbr.org/2005/07/level-5-leadership-the-triumph-of-humility-and-fierce-resolve.

CHAPTER TEN

TURN THE SECRET INTO PRACTICE

Suspend Status
Empower Each Person
Cultivate Connection
Reframe Reaction
Enforce Engagement
Triage Takeaways

You have the SECRET—that is, you have all the information you need *about* the six steps of the SECRET process. You know the importance of the sequence, and you know how vital it is to lay a foundation so that, as the conversation progresses, you have the permission and safety you need to exercise humility and apply assertiveness.

You also have the secret of the SECRET. You know that the real power of the SECRET process lies in the way it changes your conversation behavior to intentional conversation behavior. What you do not have, as of yet, is practice in *doing* conversation differently.

For some of you, to *do* conversation differently requires adding more humility to your assertiveness. You will need to *do* more suspending of status, more empowering of others, and more cultivating of connections. For others, you will need to add more assertiveness to your humility. You will need to reframe your reaction more, enforce engagement more, and triage takeaways more often and more consistently. In any case, to change your everyday conversation into an intentional conversation, you must start by identifying which SECRET steps are natural to you and which ones are not natural to you, so that you can intentionally inject them into your conversations. Let me illustrate what I mean. Take a look at the everyday conversation example below:

> **Speaker One:** "I'm not going to tell my manager that I'm not coming to work the day we have that large shipment arriving. I'm just tired of working so hard for so little pay."

> **Speaker Two:** "Oh, um . . . okay. Hey, what are you doing this weekend?"

How would you naturally respond if you were Speaker Two in this conversation? Think in terms of humility and assertiveness and the SECRET steps. If you were Speaker Two, to change this into an intentional conversation, would you choose to exercise humility or apply assertiveness? If you were to choose humility, which of the humility steps—*suspend status, empower each person,* or *cultivate connection*—would you inject? If you were to choose assertiveness, which one of the assertive steps—*reframe reaction, enforce engagement,* or *triage takeaways*—would you inject?

Whatever choices you make, remember that the SECRET is sequential. That means, for example, if you were to inject step five, *enforce engagement,* just remember that you need to have the safety and permission that comes from the previous four steps, otherwise it will negatively impact the conversation. In the example given, the two speakers are friends and, for our purposes now, let's assume that they have worked through some of the earlier steps of the process. Remember, in every conversation, we get to determine what happens next. Speaker Two, in this instance, decided not to respond directly to the subject that Speaker One was discussing. Going forward, as you practice intentional conversation, you will decide what happens next when you consider "does this conversation require humility or assertiveness from me?" In this example, Speaker Two could have made the decision to inject the assertive *enforce engagement* step. This is how that would have looked:

> **Revised Speaker Two Response:** "I hear what you are saying, but have you thought about how much work that is going to put on me?"

Okay, so that first practice session was to remind you to think first in terms of humility and assertiveness when you want to turn everyday conversation into intentional conversation. Let's continue to practice the six steps in sequence as you suggest what could be injected into the everyday conversations that follow.

STEP 1:
SUSPEND STATUS

SUSPEND STATUS: to communicate in a way that values and esteems the other person as equal to or higher than yourself.

EVERYDAY CONVERSATION #1

Speaker One: "I think I have the solution to our problem on machine number six. Is now a good time to tell you about my idea?"

Speaker Two: "I'm tired of ideas. I need action!"

DETERMINE WHICH SPEAKER NEEDS TO INJECT WHICH ACTION STEP (HUMILITY OR ASSERTIVENESS).

REVISE THIS SPEAKER'S STATEMENT SO THAT IT REFLECTS THE ACTION STEP NOTED ABOVE.

EVERYDAY CONVERSATION #1 REVISION

Speaker One: "I think I have the solution to our problem on machine number six. Is now a good time to tell you about my idea?"

Speaker Two: "I'm tired of ideas. I need action!"

DETERMINE WHICH SPEAKER NEEDS TO INJECT WHICH ACTION STEP (HUMILITY OR ASSERTIVENESS).

Speaker Two should exercise humility.

REVISE THIS SPEAKER'S STATEMENT SO THAT IT RE-FLECTS THE ACTION STEP NOTED ABOVE.

"I am very glad to hear you have a solution. I for one do not know what we would do if we can't fix the problem. Go ahead and tell me your idea so we can get to work on fixing it."

Here's the takeaway from Step 1:

There is a necessary sequence in the SECRET—whoever has status (perceived, formal, or relational) must yield that status first in order for the other person to feel safe enough to enter into an intentional conversation.

STEP 2:
EMPOWER EACH PERSON

EMPOWER EACH PERSON: to serve the other person during conversation in a way that validates that you have his or her interests and well-being in mind.

EVERYDAY CONVERSATION #2

Speaker One: "Rewrite this last paragraph—this is substandard work. My department is known for being top-notch. You will have to do better than this going forward."

Speaker Two: "This is the third time you have asked me to rewrite the same paragraph. I do not think I will ever be able to please you."

DETERMINE WHICH SPEAKER NEEDS TO INJECT WHICH ACTION STEP (HUMILITY OR ASSERTIVENESS).

REVISE THIS SPEAKER'S STATEMENT SO THAT IT REFLECTS THE ACTION STEP NOTED ABOVE.

EVERYDAY CONVERSATION #2 REVISION

Speaker One: "Rewrite this last paragraph—this is substandard work. My department is known for being topnotch. You will have to do better than this going forward."

Speaker Two: "This is the third time you have asked me to rewrite the same paragraph. I do not think I will ever be able to please you."

DETERMINE WHICH SPEAKER NEEDS TO INJECT WHICH ACTION STEP (HUMILITY OR ASSERTIVENESS).

Speaker One should exercise humility.

REVISE THIS SPEAKER'S STATEMENT SO THAT IT REFLECTS THE ACTION STEP NOTED ABOVE.

"This is the third time you have tried to give me what I need. What can I do to help you understand better what it is I expect?"

Here's the takeaway from Step 2:

This second step, *empower each person*, facilitates a new way of thinking that commits both manager and employee to serving each other. A manager practicing this step will do the unusual thing of serving the employee rather than expecting or demanding to be served.

STEP 3:
CULTIVATE CONNECTION

CULTIVATE CONNECTION: to create an environment of mutual giving and receiving in order to forge a deeper relationship.

EVERYDAY CONVERSATION #3

Speaker One: "I have been an executive coach for some of the biggest names around. I know just how to help people change—and I am pretty good at it. So what can I help you with today?"

Speaker Two: "I'm not sure. Maybe I just need some time to think about it. I'll get back to you, okay?"

DETERMINE WHICH SPEAKER NEEDS TO INJECT WHICH ACTION STEP (HUMILITY OR ASSERTIVENESS).

REVISE THIS SPEAKER'S STATEMENT SO THAT IT RE-FLECTS THE ACTION STEP NOTED ABOVE.

EVERYDAY CONVERSATION #3 REVISION

Speaker One: "I have been an executive coach for some of the biggest names around. I know just how to help people change—and I am pretty good at it. So what can I help you with today?"

Speaker Two: "I'm not sure. Maybe I just need some time to think about it. I'll get back to you, okay?"

DETERMINE WHICH SPEAKER NEEDS TO INJECT WHICH ACTION STEP (HUMILITY OR ASSERTIVENESS).

Speaker One should exercise humility.

REVISE THIS SPEAKER'S STATEMENT SO THAT IT REFLECTS THE ACTION STEP NOTED ABOVE.

"I will use whatever expertise I have to help you. Tell me what you need."

Here's the takeaway from Step 3:

People who cultivate connection demonstrate that they care for the other person during the conversation. If you were to go back to the earlier chapters and look at the people in this book who were highlighted as modeling intentional conversations, you will see that the connection deepened during their conversations, as both parties were giving and receiving. In a way, it's like the cycle of nature—as we cultivate the soil, the soil in turn nourishes the seed and returns our food back to us. To cultivate connection, the same kind of cycle is at play—you give to the other person, and he or she in turn gives to you.

STEP 4:
REFRAME REACTION

REFRAME REACTION: to manage your responses during the conversation in a way that ensures that the conversation moves forward.

EVERYDAY CONVERSATION #4

Speaker One: "I am so glad I got ahold of you. I really need to talk. Our boss is retiring and I want to apply for his job, but I found out today that you are also going to apply. I don't think you should since I am applying."

Speaker Two: "Well you know what they say—all is fair in love and war. You should keep that to yourself."

DETERMINE WHICH SPEAKER NEEDS TO INJECT WHICH ACTION STEP (HUMILITY OR ASSERTIVENESS).

REVISE THIS SPEAKER'S STATEMENT SO THAT IT REFLECTS THE ACTION STEP NOTED ABOVE.

EVERYDAY CONVERSATION #4 REVISION

Speaker One: "I am so glad I got ahold of you. I really need to talk. Our boss is retiring and I want to apply for his job, but I found out today that you are also going to apply. I don't think you should since I am applying."

Speaker Two: "Well you know what they say—all is fair in love and war. You should keep that to yourself."

DETERMINE WHICH SPEAKER NEEDS TO INJECT WHICH ACTION STEP (HUMILITY OR ASSERTIVENESS).

Speaker Two should exercise assertiveness.

REVISE THIS SPEAKER'S STATEMENT SO THAT IT REFLECTS THE ACTION STEP NOTED ABOVE.

"Why do you say that?"

Here's the takeaway from Step 4:

By taking the *reframe reaction* step, we esteem the value of a positive, free-flowing, continuous exchange. We establish that we want the conversation to continue to progress and deepen. We are also demonstrating our vested interest in building a relationship that is more than superficial—one that is durable enough to endure the unexpected twists and turns of everyday conversation.

STEP 5:
ENFORCE ENGAGEMENT

ENFORCE ENGAGEMENT: to insist that your ideas, thoughts, and information are received and acted upon.

EVERYDAY CONVERSATION #5

Speaker One:"I know exactly what you are going to say. We have been over this a thousand times and I am not interested in hearing the same thing from you again."

Speaker Two: "If that's how you feel about it, I will just leave it alone."

DETERMINE WHICH SPEAKER NEEDS TO INJECT WHICH ACTION STEP (HUMILITY OR ASSERTIVENESS).

REVISE THIS SPEAKER'S STATEMENT SO THAT IT RE-FLECTS THE ACTION STEP NOTED ABOVE.

EVERYDAY CONVERSATION #5 REVISION

Speaker One: "I know exactly what you are going to say. We have been over this a thousand times and I am not interested in hearing the same thing from you again."

Speaker Two: "If that's how you feel about it, I will just leave it alone."

DETERMINE WHICH SPEAKER NEEDS TO INJECT WHICH ACTION STEP (HUMILITY OR ASSERTIVENESS).

Speaker Two should exercise assertiveness.

REVISE THIS SPEAKER'S STATEMENT SO THAT IT REFLECTS THE ACTION STEP NOTED ABOVE.

"What action have you decided to take as a result of what you have heard me say before?"

Here's the takeaway from Step 5:

When we enforce engagement, we take bold steps to be heard, and we follow through to ensure that our message is clear and is acted upon. Most conversations lack this type of boldness, and as a result, lack the clarity that is needed to change behavior. The *enforce engagement* step changes our behavior in that we say what needs to be said at the moment it needs to be said in order to get the results we need. At this stage, we challenge assumptions that are unclear or seem unfounded. We introduce ideas or information that clarify and redirect the focus of discussion. The *enforce engagement* step is where both parties get in sync with each other.

STEP 6:
TRIAGE TAKEAWAYS

TRIAGE TAKEAWAYS: to prune and select what really matters from the clutter of ideas, thoughts, and pieces of information that make up the deluge of everyday conversations.

EVERYDAY CONVERSATION #6

Speaker One: "The tasks are being done okay. Sometimes they take a little long, but I suppose that should be expected due to the perfection the client is requiring these days. I just wished there was a way to meet more of the deadlines. Then, of course, the union has been very verbal about work load and overtime hours."

Speaker Two: "I am going to continue working hard to get things done at the highest degree of perfection as possible."

DETERMINE WHICH SPEAKER NEEDS TO INJECT WHICH ACTION STEP (HUMILITY OR ASSERTIVENESS).

REVISE THIS SPEAKER'S STATEMENT SO THAT IT REFLECTS THE ACTION STEP NOTED ABOVE.

EVERYDAY CONVERSATION #6 REVISION

Speaker One: "The tasks are being done okay. Sometimes they take a little long, but I suppose that should be expected due to the perfection the client is requiring these days. I just wished there was a way to meet more of the deadlines. Then, of course, the union has been very verbal about work load and overtime hours."

Speaker Two: "I am going to continue working hard to get things done at the highest degree of perfection as possible."

DETERMINE WHICH SPEAKER NEEDS TO INJECT WHICH ACTION STEP (HUMILITY OR ASSERTIVENESS).

Speaker Two should exercise assertiveness.

REVISE THIS SPEAKER'S STATEMENT SO THAT IT REFLECTS THE ACTION STEP NOTED ABOVE.

"What is most important to you? How do you think we need to adjust to meet more deadlines?"

Here's the takeaway from Step 6:

This last step, *triage takeaways*, adds intent to the way we prune and select what really matters from the clutter of ideas, thoughts, and pieces of information that make up the deluge of everyday conversations. Becoming intentionally selective and precise about which conversations (and what ideas within a conversation) deserve more or less of your energy is critical to your success as an employee, manager, parent, priest, or person.

ULTIMATELY, TO HAVE AN INTENTIONAL CONVERSATION, WE NEED TO EXERCISE HUMILITY AND APPLY ASSERTIVENESS.

Humility is required when we suspend status, empower each other, and cultivate connections.

Assertiveness is required when we reframe our reactions, enforce engagement, and triage takeaways.

Conversation is a word with many meanings and applications. At times, a conversation is a brief chat with another person. At other times, a conversation is a longer, more serious exchange. A conversation can also be when you are called to the principal's office, or sitting before your manager, or when your spouse says, "Honey, we need to talk." For those of us at TAG, conversation is a tool by which to serve others. It is a tool for you, too—even a powerful tool—once you become intentional in using it to transform your career and your relationships. And you can do that—_will_ do that—by using the SECRET process to turn everyday conversation into intentional conversations.

ABOUT THE AUTHOR

KEN TUCKER is a highly sought-after speaker, trusted advisor, and chief designer of the Intentional Difference Process. He is co-author of *Animals, Inc: A Business Parable for the 21st Century* (Warner Books, February 2004) and author of *Are You Fascinated? The Four People You Need to Succeed* (Dailey Swann Publishing, August 2009), and coauthor of *The Leadership Triangle* and *Your Intentional Difference: One Word Changes Everything.*

As a thought leader, Ken Tucker brings many years of experience as a speaker and principle consultant, formerly with The Gallup Organization, then as strategic consultant and CEO of Ken Tucker and Associates, LLC, and now senior partner at TAG Consulting. With TAG, Ken serves as a leadership strategist and executive coach for chief officers in Fortune 500 companies and government agencies in the United States, Mexico, United Kingdom, and Australia. Ken has shared speaking platforms with Colin Powell, Jim Collins, and Marcus Buckingham and is a regular contributor to management columns. Ken and his family live in Virginia.

ABOUT FAMILIUS

Welcome to a place where parents are celebrated, not compared. Where heart is at the center of our families, and family at the center of our homes. Where boo-boos are still kissed, cake beaters are still licked, and mistakes are still okay. Welcome to a place where books— and family—are beautiful. Familius: a book publisher dedicated to helping families be happy.

VISIT OUR WEBSITE: WWW.FAMILIUS.COM

Our website is a different kind of place. Get inspired, read articles, discover books, watch videos, connect with our family experts, download books and apps and audiobooks, and along the way, discover how values and happy family life go together.

JOIN OUR FAMILY

There are lots of ways to connect with us! Subscribe to our newsletters at www.familius.com to receive uplifting daily inspiration, essays from our Pater Familius, a free ebook every month, and the first word on special discounts and Familius news.

BECOME AN EXPERT

Familius authors and other established writers interested in helping families be happy are invited to join our family and contribute online content. If you have something important to say on the family, join our expert community by applying at:

www.familius.com/apply-to-become-a-familius-expert

GET BULK DISCOUNTS

THE MOST IMPORTANT WORK YOU EVER DO WILL BE WITHIN THE WALLS OF YOUR OWN HOME.

CPSIA information can be obtained
at www.ICGtesting.com
Printed in the USA
FFOW04n1140010318
45353008-46039FF